W9-BOD-669

THE POCKET DICTIONARY OF SIGNING

ROD R. BUTTERWORTH
and
MICKEY FLODIN

A PERIGEE BOOK

*Dedicated to all who are willing to make the effort
to learn sign language and, by so doing, to enrich and
enlarge the lives of the hearing and nonhearing alike.*

Also by Rod R. Butterworth and Mickey Flodin

THE PERIGEE VISUAL DICTIONARY OF SIGNING

Perigee Books
are published by
The Putnam Publishing Group
200 Madison Avenue
New York, NY 10016

Copyright © 1987 by Rod R. Butterworth and Mickey Flodin
All rights reserved. This book, or parts thereof,
may not be reproduced in any form without permission.
Published simultaneously in Canada by
General Publishing Co. Limited, Toronto

Library of Congress Cataloging-in-Publication Data

Butterworth, Rod R.
  The pocket dictionary of signing.

  Rev. ed. of: The Perigee visual dictionary of
signing. c1983.
  Includes index.
  1. Sign language—Dictionaries. I. Flodin,
Mickey. II. Butterworth, Rod R.   Perigee visual
dictionary of signing. III. Title.
HV2475.B87   1987   419'.03'21   86-25596
ISBN 0-399-51347-7

Printed in the United States of America
9   10

Contents

Acknowledgments

The Pocket Dictionary of Signing has become a reality because of the willing cooperation of many people. If it were not for the vision and compassionate concern of certain individuals for the deaf and the hearing impaired, our original dictionary and this pocket dictionary would have been supremely more difficult to complete. But, happily, there *are* such compassionate and caring people in the world, and it has been our privilege to work with some of them during the preparation of this work. Special thanks are due to:

Lynn Lutjen, instructor in deaf education for the Department of Speech and Theater, Southwest Missouri State University, Springfield, Missouri. Her willingness to act as a consultant from the early stages of the development of this dictionary has resulted in many profitable suggestions concerning the descriptions and illustrations.

Marybeth Herens, instructor of reading and language at Colorado State School for the Deaf and Blind, Colorado Springs, Colorado. Her expertise in sign language and language disciplines has provided valuable input throughout the preparation of this dictionary.

Many deaf friends and interpreters for the deaf, who have given encouragement and advice along the way.

Christine Butterworth, for assistance in typing and correcting the manuscript.

Joanna Butterworth, for moral support as a devoted wife and sacrificial giving of her time to editing and correcting the manuscript.

Barbara J. Holland, for her valuable editorial suggestions regarding the improvement of the text, and many hours spent proofreading.

The rest of the Butterworth family, who all shared in the work at various stages: Winifred Butterworth, Michael, Donna, and Geoffrey.

Carol Flodin, for her enthusiasm and for her extensive labors in numerous ways during the production of this book.

Daniel Flodin, who helped when he could and who waited patiently for his dad to return to a more normal schedule.

—R.R.B.
—M.F.

Introduction

THIS DICTIONARY is unique in that, to our knowledge, it is the first time such a text for American Sign Language has been produced in a pocket-sized edition. The smaller physical size has obvious advantages in convenience of handling, carrying about on one's person or keeping in a car glove compartment, or even for sending copies through the mail.

The Pocket Dictionary of Signing is derived from a larger and more comprehensive work, *The Perigee Visual Dictionary of Signing*. However, many people need a smaller, economical, and more concise volume—yet one that still provides an ample vocabulary for effective communication. Careful research has been carried out to discover which everyday English words are the most widely used on the North American continent. Thus this present dictionary came into being.

There are approximately fourteen million hearing-impaired people in the United States. About two million of this number are classified as deaf. Deaf people look with favor upon those who seek to learn their language and will have patience and understanding with the beginning signer. American Sign Language is not difficult to learn. The student or person interested in learning sign language will pick up a great deal from this dictionary alone. In addition, sign language classes are becoming more and more prevalent in universities and colleges.

One must realize that just as the English language is constantly changing and developing, so is the sign language of the deaf. New signs are constantly being created and developed within the deaf community. These often spread across the country and become widely accepted.

The purpose of this dictionary is to provide a starting point. The signs included have been chosen because they are commonly known and accepted by the majority of people who use signs. Even so, there will always be those who have special preferences concerning the way to make a particular sign.

Communicating effectively with the deaf is the goal that all concerned people—friends, relatives, and the hearing impaired—aim for. We trust that this volume will be a useful tool toward the achievement of that end.

A Brief History

WHO INVENTED sign language? No one knows for certain, but the most likely answer is that the deaf themselves were the ones who, out of necessity, created a variety of gestures in order to communicate with each other. Of course, different groups of deaf people in diverse geographical locations developed their own unique methods of sign language.

In the ancient world when children were discovered to be deaf they were often disowned and left to die or fend for themselves. During the Middle Ages there was a limited amount of sign language communication in European countries, but this was mainly in connection with monasteries, especially those where vows of silence were imposed.

One must assume that as far as America is concerned, the deaf quickly developed their own methods of communication by signing. For example, Martha's Vineyard, an island in southeastern Massachusetts, was settled as early as 1642 and remained somewhat culturally isolated for the next couple of hundred years. Quite a significant deaf population developed on the island. It is interesting that both the deaf and the hearing-speaking people of Martha's Vineyard used sign language as a method of communication. Of course, we must recognize the influence and contribution made by more heterogeneous deaf immigrants who came from the Old World, as well. All contributed in varying degrees to what is known today as American Sign Language, or ASL.

It was in the early nineteenth century that sign language as we know it today was officially brought to the United States. This was due to the interest and efforts of a young Congregational minister in Connecticut named Thomas Hopkins Gallaudet. Gallaudet traveled to Europe and returned with Laurent Clerc, a deaf sign-language teacher from Paris, France. They worked together and developed an American sign language based on the French system.

Soon schools for the deaf began to appear in several states. In 1864, Gallaudet College was established in Washington, D.C. Gallaudet continues to the present day as a fine liberal arts college for the deaf.

Interest in sign language continues to grow among the hearing population of North America, and American Sign Language is now the fourth most used language in the United States.

How to Use This Dictionary

1. USE OF THE ALPHABET

The first step in learning sign language is mastery of the manual alphabet. (See the section on page 11.) The easiest and most generally accepted method of explaining sign movements incorporates the use of hand shapes that are often related to particular letters in the manual alphabet.

For example, the expression "right *B* hand" indicates the right hand in the position for signing the letter *B*. All similar expressions follow the same procedure unless a variation is specified in the text.

2. TERMS RELATED TO BASIC HAND POSITIONS

The following illustrations portray the basic terminology that is used to explain the various hand shapes and positions.

A. *AND* HAND

Note that unless otherwise stated, the expression refers only to the ending position of the *and* hand as it is here illustrated.

B. FLAT HAND

The fingers are touching unless otherwise indicated by the addition of a term such as flat *open* hand.

C. CURVED HAND

The fingers are touching unless otherwise indicated by the addition of a term such as curved *open* hand.

D. OPEN HAND

E. CLOSED HAND

F. BENT HAND

G. CLAWED HAND

3. DIRECTION AND ORIENTATION OF ILLUSTRATIONS

The illustrations show what is seen when another person faces you and you observe that person signing. It is *not* the same as looking into a mirror, for then the right hand would appear to be the left hand.

Some of the illustrations are drawn from an angle or profile perspective. In many cases this has been for the purpose of making the illustration clearer and easier to understand.

4. ARROWS

Great care has been taken to guide the student's comprehension of a sign movement by the use of arrows. However, it is sometimes possible to perceive a different movement from the actual one in question if the reader is not extremely careful. Read the descriptions thoroughly when you are learning a new sign. They will guide and aid the beginning sign language student in understanding the correct movement.

5. CLOCKWISE, COUNTERCLOCKWISE

Unless otherwise stated, these terms are to be understood from the viewpoint of the signer, not the observer.

6. INFLECTIONS

Following are some of the word endings commonly used. They may be added to the basic sign for more exact expression when appropriate.

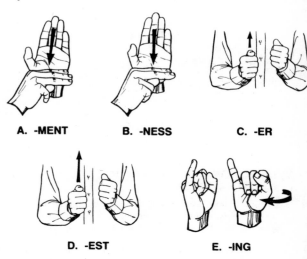

A. -MENT   B. -NESS   C. -ER

D. -EST   E. -ING

7. MEMORY AIDS

The addition of memory aids will help the beginning student retain and recall the signs with their positions and movements. The memory aids are not necessarily related to what may be considered the origin of a sign.

8. MAIN ENTRY AND SYNONYM INDEX

The Main Entry and Synonym Index is a list of all the main entry words and all the synonyms following the main entries. The sign language student will find this list a rich resource and an invaluable aid to versatility of expression. Remember to check the index at the end of this dictionary if you do not find a word you are looking for. It could be a synonym of another lead word. For a more comprehensive vocabulary see *The Perigee Visual Dictionary of Signing*.

The Manual Alphabet

1. THE SIGNS

The right hand is generally used to form the letters of the alphabet, although the left hand can also be used. They are illustrated as seen by the observer, or in some cases at a slightly different angle for the sake of clarity. Generally speaking, the hand should be held comfortably at shoulder level and in front of the body, with the palm facing forward.

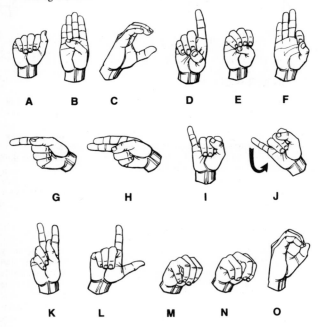

A B C D E F

G H I J

K L M N O

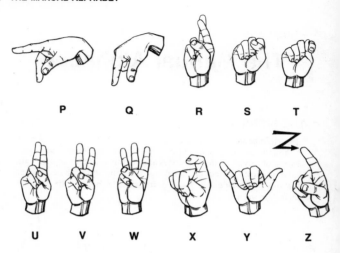

P Q R S T

U V W X Y Z

2. FINGERSPELLING

Once the manual alphabet has been mastered, the beginner can practice spelling words letter by letter. Fingerspelling is constantly used among the deaf to communicate words for which there are no signs, especially names of people and places. But the beginning signer can freely use fingerspelling to spell a word that he or she does not yet know the sign for. Remember, communication is the goal, and fingerspelling will get your message through.

Practice fingerspelling the following words and simple sentences.

TWO-LETTER WORDS

am	on	be	to
it	go	at	up
or	if	an	by
he	we	do	in
as	hi	so	

THREE-LETTER WORDS

yet	new	mud	hit
Tim	Joe	big	but
old	Sam	cat	son
Bob	gas	pen	car
Dan	pig	van	toe
Ted	may	not	fix
Pam	saw	rat	hot
fig	elm	dog	kit
Jan	zoo	let	

FOUR-LETTER WORDS

land	some	seen	cent
bang	weak	vain	sank
sink	felt	pack	last
near	leap	goat	vote
meat	bean	zone	line
keep	walk	date	ship
rope	sent	salt	when
dare	king	cash	grip
lake	ream	more	
meet	dock		

WORDS WITH FIVE LETTERS OR MORE

please	blink	sleep
twelve	drown	chair
spring	brilliant	prayer
trust	cloudy	fruit
fling	teach	swept
school	smile	street
dwindle	skirt	
phrase	cream	

MORE ADVANCED WORDS

available	indirect	joyful
worthless	disagree	positive
personal	goodness	encompass
deafness	precede	complete
review	appearance	untrue
excite	conflict	development
going	action	costly
program		

SENTENCES (TO SIGN A QUESTION, SEE P. 127)

I LIVE IN NEW YORK.
MY MOTHER WENT SHOPPING.
WHERE ARE THE STUDENTS?
WE HAVE TWO APPLE TREES.
SPRING HAS ARRIVED.
WE BOUGHT THREE PUPPIES.
I HAVE AN OLD CAR.
IT'S TOO HOT TO PLAY.
HAVE YOU BEEN TO NEW MEXICO?
SHE WENT TO FRANCE LAST YEAR.
MARY LIVES NEXT DOOR.
WHAT TIME IS IT?
KEVIN HAS NEW SHOES.
PLEASE SIGN SLOWLY AND CLEARLY.
MY UNCLE JACK VISITED CHICAGO LAST WEEK.

Numbers

THE RIGHT PALM generally faces forward unless otherwise indicated by illustration or description.

1. ZERO TO A MILLION

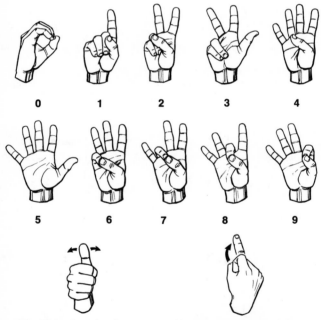

0	**1**	**2**	**3**	**4**
5	**6**	**7**	**8**	**9**

10 Shake the *A* hand.

11 Flick the right index finger up with palm facing self.

12 Flick the right index and middle finger up with palm facing forward.

13 Move the fingers of the right *3* hand up and down with palm facing self.

14 Move the fingers of the right *4* hand up and down with palm facing self.

15 Move the fingers of the right *5* hand up and down with palm facing self.

16 Sign *10*, then *6*.

17 Sign *10*, then *7*.

18 Sign *10*, then *8*.

19 Sign *10*, then *9*.

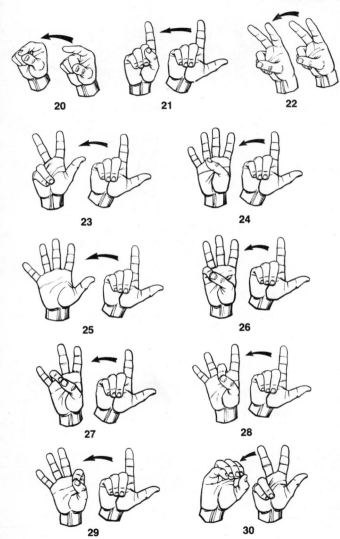

20

21

22

23

24

25

26

27

28

29

30

HUNDRED Sign *1*, then *C*.   **THOUSAND** Bring the right *M*
fingertips down into
the left flat hand.

MILLION Bring the right *M* fingertips
down into the left flat palm
twice.

2. FRACTIONS

Sign the upper half of the fraction first, then lower the hand a short
distance and sign the lower half.

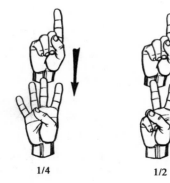

1/4   1/2   3/5

3. MONEY

A. CENTS

1¢   8¢

B. DOLLARS

The palm faces forward, then dips and turns so that the palm faces self.

$1.00

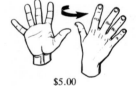

$5.00 $9.00

4. NUMBERS FOR PRACTICE

8	77	346	716	6,347
10	89	371	753	9,219
17	94	482	891	15,413
23	122	423	838	17,526
35	139	555	964	39,892
48	174	548	939	1,324,948
52	293	601	1,549	43,268,512
61	227	686	4,858	579,643,810

Phrases

HERE ARE some examples of how you can form simple phrases and sentences by using the signs from this dictionary. As your skill in signing increases, remember that appropriate facial expressions and bodily gestures are just as important, if not more so, as in verbal communication. Bear in mind that the majority of signs are performed in the upper torso and head area. This aids the deaf person by making it easier to observe the mouth for combining lipreading with interpretation of the sign.

PHRASES

HI.
WHAT IS YOUR NAME?
MY NAME IS D-A-N-I-E-L.
HOW ARE YOU?
I'M FINE, THANK YOU.
I'M SORRY.
PLEASE EXCUSE ME.
YOU'RE WELCOME.
I'M HUNGRY.
I LOVE YOU.
HELP ME.
I DON'T KNOW.
HAVE A NICE DAY.

Hi.

What

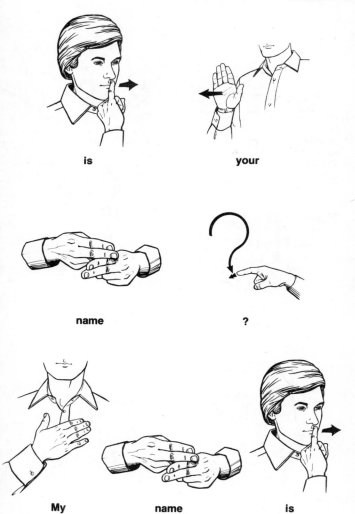

is

your

name

?

My

name

is

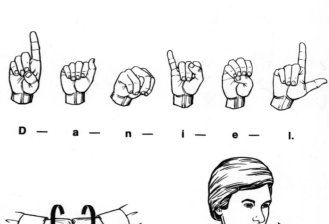

D — a — n — i — e — l.

How

are

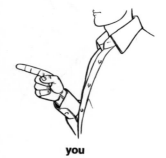

you

?

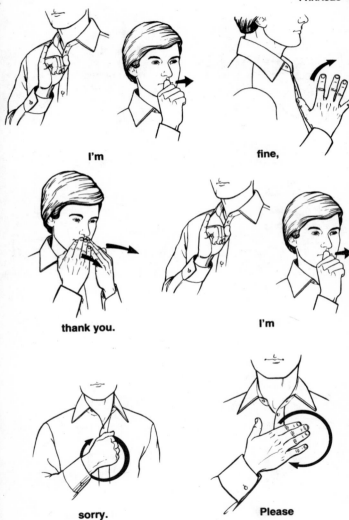

I'm

fine,

thank you.

I'm

sorry.

Please

excuse

me.

You're welcome.

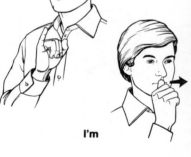

I'm

hungry.

I love you.

Help

me.

I

don't know.

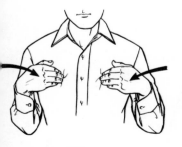

Have

a

nice

day.

A

ABOVE, OVER

Make a counterclockwise circle with the right flat hand over the left flat hand.

Memory aid: Suggests one level that is *higher* than another.

Examples: He is honest and *above* deception. She has authority *over* thirty assistants.

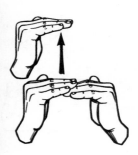

ABOVE (comparative degree), EXCEED, MORE THAN, OVER

Hold both bent hands to the front of the body with the right fingers on top of the left fingers. Raise the bent right hand a short distance. *Note:* Compare *below*.

Memory aid: The right hand moves *above* the left hand.

Examples: Carolyn's grades are *above* average. He took *more than* his brother.

ADD

Cross the right index finger horizontally over the left vertical index finger. *Note:* Compare *increase* and *total*.

Memory aid: Symbolizes the mathematical sign for *addition*.

Example: Please *add* 43 and 96.

AFTER

Hold the slightly curved left hand out to the front with palm facing in. Place the curved right palm on the back of the left hand and move forward and away from the left hand. *Note*: Compare *before* (time).

Memory aid: The right hand moves forward *after* touching the left.

Example: Clean the room *after* you have finished.

AFTERNOON

Hold the left arm in a horizontal position pointing to the right. The left hand is flat with palm facing down. Place the right forearm on the back of the left hand at a 45-degree angle.

Memory aid: Symbolizes the sun making its descent.

Example: Please come this *afternoon* at 4:00 P.M.

AGAIN, ENCORE, FREQUENT, OFTEN, REPEAT

Hold the left flat hand pointing forward with palm up and the bent right hand palm up and parallel to the left hand. Move the bent right hand upward and turn it over until the fingertips are placed in the left palm. Sometimes the left hand is pointed up with the palm facing right. Repeat the sign a few times to sign *frequent* and *often*.

Memory aid: Similar to a clapping action, indicating the desire for *repetition*.

Example: I will visit London *again*.

AGAINST, OPPOSE

Thrust the fingertips of the right flat hand into the palm of the left flat hand.

Memory aid: Suggests one hand attacking the other.

Example: I am *opposed* to his decision.

AGREE, ACCORD, COINCIDE, CONSENT, CORRESPOND

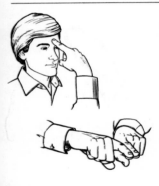

Touch the forehead with the right index finger; then move both *D* hands to chest level with palms down and sides of index fingers touching. The latter is the sign for *same*.

Memory aid: A meeting of minds in unison.

Examples: So you *agree*? Let's be in *accord* about this. Does Richard *consent* to the new plan? The information doesn't *correspond*.

ALL, ENTIRE, WHOLE

Hold the left flat hand to the front with palm facing the body. Move the right flat hand, with palm facing out, over-down-in-up, ending with the back of the right hand in the palm of the left hand.

Memory aid: The circular action suggests an encompassing and a completeness.

Example: The board members *all* agreed.

ALL RIGHT, OK

Hold the left flat hand with palm facing
up. Move the little-finger edge of the right
flat hand across the face of the left hand
from the heel to the fingertips. *OK* is
often fingerspelled.

Memory aid: The movement suggests a
straight line with agreement to move
ahead.

Examples: Your plan seems *all right* to us.
It's *OK* with me.

ALWAYS, CONSTANTLY, EVER

Point the right index finger forward-
upward with palm up, then move it in a
clockwise circle.

Memory aid: The circle suggests continu-
ance.

Example: That boy is *always* getting into
trouble.

AM, ARE, BE, IS

Place the right *A*-hand thumb on the lips
and move the right hand straight forward.
The other verbs are made with the same
movement forward from the lips but are
individually initialized. Use *R* for *are*, *B*
for *be*, and *I* for *is*.

Memory aid: Indicates a breathing person
and thus a symbolic connection with the
verb *to be*.

Examples: I *am* going. They *are* clever. *Be*
careful. What *is* that?

AMERICA

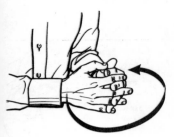

Interlock the fingers of both slightly curved open hands and move them from right to left in an outward circle.

Memory aid: The interlocked fingers suggest the log fences made by *America's* early settlers.

Example: America is blessed with abundant resources.

AND

Place the right open hand in front with palm facing in and fingers pointing to the left. Move the hand to the right while bringing the fingertips and thumb together.

Memory aid: Symbolizes a stretching action. The conjunction *and* stretches sentences.

Example: Please make biscuits *and* gravy.

ANGER, FUME, RAGE, WRATH

Place the fingertips of both curved hands against the abdomen and draw them forcefully up to the chest with slight inward curves.

Memory aid: Suggests *angry* feelings rising from within.

Examples: He *fumed* inwardly. Dan's *rage* seemed unabatable.

ANIMAL

Place the fingertips of both bent hands on the chest. Maintain the position of the fingertips while rocking both hands in and out sideways.

Memory aid: Suggests the often pronounced breathing movements of an animal that has exerted itself physically.

Example: Donna is a real *animal* lover.

ANSWER, REPLY, RESPOND

Hold the right vertical index finger to the lips and place the left vertical index finger a short distance in front. Pivot both hands forward and down from the wrists so that the index fingers point forward.

Memory aid: Suggests an *answer* coming from the mouth.

Example: Give him your *answer* now.

ANY, ANYBODY, ANYONE, ANYTHING, THING, SUBSTANCE

Place the right *A* hand in front of the body with the palm facing in. Swing it to the right with the palm facing forward. Add the numerical sign for *one* when signing *anybody* or *anyone*. Add the movement of dropping the right flat hand slightly a few times while moving it to the right when signing *anything*, *thing*, and *substance*.

Memory aid: The hand seems to be searching for *something* and suggesting alternatives.

Examples: Does he know *anybody* here?
Do you have *anything* we can use?

ANYWAY, ANYHOW, ALTHOUGH, DOESN'T MATTER, NO MATTER, REGARDLESS

Hold both slightly curved hands to the front with palms facing up and fingertips pointing toward each other. Brush the fingertips back and forth over each other a few times.

Memory aid: A vague type of action that suggests many possibilities.

Examples: No matter what you say, I am going. It *doesn't matter* to me.

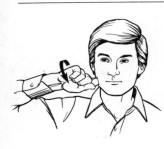

APPLE

Pivot the knuckle of the right closed index finger back and forth on the right cheek. *Alternative* (not illustrated): The right *A* thumb is sometimes used.

Memory aid: Can relate to the expression Rosy red cheeks, which reminds one of *apples*.

Example: The *apples* were cheap.

AS

Point both index fingers forward together with a short distance between them and the palms facing down. Maintain this position as both hands are moved to the left. *Note*: Compare *same* and *too*.

Memory aid: The repeated action indicates something extra or added.

Examples: The air felt as hot *as* a furnace.

ASK, REQUEST

Bring both flat hands together with palms touching and move them in a backward arc toward the body.

Memory aid: Suggests the traditional hand position of a person engaged in prayer.

Example: I'll *ask* my boss for a raise.

AT

Bring the fingers of the right flat hand in contact with the back of the left flat hand. This sign is often fingerspelled.

Memory aid: Suggests a meeting point.

Example: Meet me *at* school tomorrow.

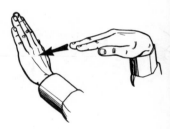

ATTEMPT, EFFORT, TRY

Hold both *A* hands to the front with palms facing; then move them forward with a pushing motion. *Effort* and *try* may be initialized.

Memory aid: Pushing takes *effort*.

Example: Will you *attempt* to race again?

AUNT

Place the right *A* hand close to the right cheek and shake back and forth from the wrist.

Memory aid: The initial *A* is placed near the *female* sign position.

Example: His *aunt* likes to baby-sit.

AWAKE, AROUSE, WAKE UP

Place the closed thumbs and index fingers of both *Q* hands at the corners of the eyes; then open eyes and fingers simultaneously.

Memory aid: Symbolizes the eyes opening.

Example: It's time to *wake up*.

B

BABY, DOLL, INFANT

Hold the arms in the natural position for cradling a baby and rock the arms sideways. *Note*: Compare *fool* as an alternative sign for *doll*.

Memory aid: The natural movement of comforting a *baby* in the arms.

Examples: She was a cute *baby*. Mary has carefully preserved her *dolls*. *Infants* up to age two will be provided for by the company nursery.

BAD

Place the fingertips of the right flat hand at the lips; then move the right hand down and turn it so that the palm faces down.

Memory aid: Suggests something that has been tasted and disapproved of.

Example: This fruit has gone *bad*.

BASEBALL, BAT, SOFTBALL

Place the right *S* hand above the left *S* hand and swing them forward together from the right of the body to the center of the body.

Memory aid: The position and action of a *baseball* batter.

Example: Professional *baseball* players have to practice a lot.

BATH, BATHE

Rub both *A* hands up and down on the chest several times.

Memory aid: Symbolizes washing the body.

Example: She loved to take long, relaxing *baths*.

BEAUTIFUL, ATTRACTIVE, LOVELY, PRETTY, HANDSOME

Place the fingertips of the right *and* hand at the chin and open the hand as it describes a counterclockwise circle around the face. The *H* hand can be used when signing *handsome*.

Memory aid: The circular movement suggests symmetrical or balanced facial features.

Example: You have an *attractive* daughter.

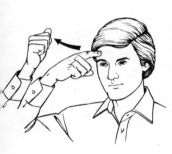

BECAUSE

Place the right index finger on the forehead. Move slightly to the right and upward while forming the *A* hand.

Memory aid: Touching the forehead can indicate the thought that there is a reason for everything.

Example: I appreciate you *because* you are honest.

BED

Hold both hands palm to palm and place the back of the left hand on the right cheek. *Alternative* (not illustrated): Place the slightly curved right hand on the right cheek and tilt the head to the right.

Memory aid: Both signs symbolize resting the head on a pillow.

Example: It's time to go to *bed*.

BEFORE (time)

Hold the slightly curved left hand out to the front with palm facing in. Hold the right curved hand near the palm of the left and then draw the right hand in toward the body. *Note:* Compare *after*.

Memory aid: The right hand is *before* the palm of the left.

Example: Let me read that book *before* you return it.

BELIEVE

Touch the forehead with the right index finger; then bring the right hand down until it clasps left hand in front of chest.

Memory aid: Suggests that belief is something to be held onto.

Example: Do you *believe* her story?

BELOW, BENEATH, UNDER

Make a counterclockwise circle with the right flat hand below the left flat hand. *Note*: *Under* is also signed by moving the right *A* hand under the left flat hand, and sometimes by circling the *A* hand counterclockwise in that position.

Memory aid: Suggests one level lower than another.

Example: The water remained *below* his knees.

BELOW (comparative degree), LESS THAN, UNDER

Hold both bent hands to the front with the left fingers on top of the right fingers. Lower the right hand a short distance. *Note:* Compare *above*.

Memory aid: The right hand moves *below* the left hand.

Examples: Earl's estimate was *below* his competitor's. The temperature is *less than* 30 degrees.

BEST

Touch the lips with the fingers of the right flat hand; then, while closing it into an *A*-hand shape, move it to the right side of the head above head level. *Note:* See *better*.

Memory aid: Suggests tasting something and giving a thumbs-up sign of approval.

Example: It's the *best* store for novelties that I know of.

BETTER

Touch the lips with the fingers of the right flat hand; then move it to the right side of the head while forming an *A* hand. *Note:* See *best*.

Memory aid: Suggests tasting something and giving a thumbs-up sign of approval.

Example: This year's concert was *better* than previous ones.

BETWEEN

Put the little-finger edge of the right flat hand between the thumb and index finger of the left flat hand. Pivot the right hand back and forth while keeping the right little-finger edge anchored.

Memory aid: The right hand is *between* two sides.

Example: Put the table *between* the two windows.

BICYCLE, CYCLE, TRICYCLE

Move both downturned *S* hands forward in alternate circles.

Memory aid: Symbolizes the action of pedaling a *bicycle*.

Example: Riding a *bicycle* is good for the health.

BIRTH, BIRTHDAY, BORN

Place the back of the right flat hand into the upturned left palm (right hand may start from a position near stomach). Move both hands forward and upward together. When signing *birthday*, add the sign for *day*.

Memory aid: The right hand can symbolize a baby which is presented to the left hand, and then to all.

Example: Helen gave *birth* two weeks early.

BLACK

Move the right index finger sideways across the right eyebrow.

Memory aid: Suggests the cosmetic makeup of the eyebrow.

Example: I need some *black* shoes.

BLUE

Move the right *B* hand to the right while shaking it from the wrist.

Memory aid: The initial indicates the meaning.

Example: My new shirt is *blue*.

BODY, PHYSICAL

Place the palms of both flat hands against the chest and repeat a little lower. Sometimes one hand is used.

Memory aid: The hands feel the *body*.

Example: My *body* is bruised.

BOOK, TEXTBOOK, VOLUME

Place the hands palm to palm, with fingers pointing forward. Open both hands to the palm-up position while maintaining contact with the little fingers.

Memory aid: Pictures the opening of a *book*.

Examples: Don't forget your *book*. Study your *textbook*. Please give me *volume* two.

BORING, DULL, MONOTONOUS, TEDIOUS

Touch the side of the nose with the right index finger and twist forward slightly. Assume an appropriate facial expression.

Memory aid: Shutting off the airflow of the nose suggests there is nothing interesting to smell.

Example: They found the trip *dull*.

BOY

First sign *man;* then move the right flat hand with palm facing down to waist level to indicate the height of a boy.

Memory aid: Indicate a *boy*'s height.

Example: That *boy* can swim well.

BREAD

Draw the little-finger edge of the right hand downward a few times over the back of the flat left hand which has its palm facing the body.

Memory aid: Symbolizes cutting slices of *bread*.

Example: I'd like my *bread* toasted.

BREAK, FRACTURE, SNAP

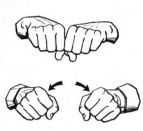

Hold the thumb and index-finger sides of both *S* hands together; then twist them both sharply outward and apart.

Memory aid: Can symbolize *breaking* a stick.

Example: The glass was *broken*. The window cord *snapped*.

BREAKFAST

Move the fingers of the right closed *and* hand to the mouth a few times. Place the left flat hand into the bend of the right elbow; then raise the right forearm upward. *Note*: This sign is a combination of *eat* and *morning*.

Memory aid: The nighttime fast is broken by eating in the morning.

Example: I did not feel hungry at *breakfast* time.

BRING, FETCH

Hold both open hands to the front with palms facing up and one hand slightly in front of the other. Move both hands toward self, another, or to the right or left, depending on who is indicated.

Memory aid: Symbolizes something being *brought* closer.

Example: Please *bring* my umbrella.

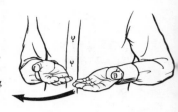

BROTHER

First sign *man,* then, with one movement, point both index fingers forward and bring them together. The latter is the sign for *same.*

Memory aid: The two signs combined suggest a male of the same family.

Example: His *brother* is a good worker.

BUT, ALTHOUGH, HOWEVER

Cross both index fingers with palms facing out; then draw them apart a short distance. *Note:* See *different.*

Memory aid: Indicates that an opposite or alternative suggestion may be forthcoming.

Example: Boxing is an exciting *but* dangerous sport. Judy is efficient; *however,* Elaine is even more so.

BUTTER

Quickly brush the fingertips of the right *H* hand across the left palm a few times.

Memory aid: Suggests spreading *butter* on bread.

Example: Put plenty of *butter* on my muffin.

BUY, PURCHASE

Move the back of the right *and* hand down into the upturned palm of the left hand, then up and straight out or slightly to the right.

Memory aid: Symbolizes laying down and giving out money for a *purchase*.

Example: Let's *buy* new furniture.

C

CAKE

Move the fingertips and thumb of the right *C* hand forward across the left flat hand from wrist to fingertips.

Memory aid: Suggests sliding a piece of *cake* from a serving dish onto someone's plate.

Example: Thank you for my birthday *cake*.

CALL, SUMMON

Place fingers of right slightly curved hand on the back of the left flat hand. Pull right hand up toward the body while forming an *A* hand. *Alternative* (not illustrated): Place the right curved hand around the mouth with palm facing left.

Memory aid: The first sign indicates that deaf persons may need to be touched to get their attention. The alternative sign is the natural gesture of cupping the mouth to project the voice.

Example: Joan was *called* to the front.

CAN, ABILITY, ABLE, CAPABLE, COMPETENT, COULD, POSSIBLE

Hold both *S* (or *A*) hands to the front and move them down firmly together.

Memory aid: The firmness of the action indicates assurance of *ability*.

Examples: I know you *can* do it. He is a *competent* instructor.

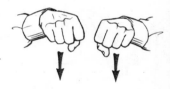

CANDY, SUGAR

Brush the tips of the right *U* fingers downward over the lips and chin a few times. *Note:* Compare *sweet*.

Memory aid: Suggests tasting something sweet.

Example: Too much *candy* is not good for your teeth.

CANNOT, IMPOSSIBLE, UNABLE, INCAPABLE

Strike the left index finger with the right index finger as it makes a downward movement. The left index maintains its position.

Memory aid: The left index *cannot* be moved.

Example: I *cannot* speak French.

CAR, AUTOMOBILE, DRIVE

Use both closed hands to manipulate an imaginary steering wheel.

Memory aid: Holding a steering wheel.

Example: Please wash the *car*. I'm learning to *drive*.

CARELESS, RECKLESS, THOUGHTLESS

Place the right *V* hand in front of the forehead with palm facing left. Move back and forth across the forehead a few times.

Memory aid: The *V* hand can suggest a mind void of common sense.

Example: He was fired for *careless* driving.

CAT

Place the index fingers and thumbs of the *F* hands under the nose with the palms facing, then move them out sideways. This sign may also be done with the right hand only.

Memory aid: Suggests a *cat*'s whiskers.

Example: I used to own a *cat* named Tiger.

CELEBRATION, CHEER, TRIUMPH, VICTORY, HALLELUJAH

Hold up one or both closed hands with the thumb tips and index fingertips touching. Make small circular movements. The *V* hands can be used for *victory*. When signing *hallelujah*, clap the hands once, then proceed with the basic sign.

Memory aid: Symbolizes the waving of small flags.

Example: The crowd *cheered* loudly.

CHEAP, INEXPENSIVE

Hold the left flat hand with fingers pointing forward and palm facing right. Brush the index-finger side of the slightly curved right hand downward across the palm of the left hand.

Memory aid: Something brushed off easily cannot be of great consequence.

Example: I bought this lamp *cheap* at a sale.

CHILD, CHILDREN

Place the right flat downturned hand before the body and motion as if patting the head of a child. When referring to more than one child, move the hand to another position and repeat the sign.

Memory aid: *Children* are shorter than adults.

Examples: Geoffrey is an exceptional *child*. The *children* like their new teacher.

CHOCOLATE

Make a few small counterclockwise circles with the thumb of the right *C* hand over the back of the left flat hand.

Memory aid: The *C* hand indicates the word, and the action suggests mixing *chocolate* icing.

Example: Chocolate cake is my favorite dessert.

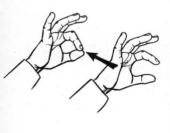

CHOOSE, PICK, SELECT

Use the right thumb and index finger to make a picking motion from the front as the hand is drawn back toward self. The remaining right fingers are extended. Sometimes the fingers of the left hand are held up in front of the right, and the right appears to be deciding which finger to choose. *Note:* Compare *find*.

Memory aid: An item is *selected* with great care.

Example: Bill *chose* the blue suit.

CHRISTMAS

Move the right *C* hand in a sideways arc
to the right with the palm facing forward.

Memory aid: The initialized movement requires context and simultaneous lipreading
for full comprehension.

Example: What does Susan want for
Christmas?

CHURCH, CHAPEL, DENOMINATION

Place the thumb of the right *C* hand on
the back of the closed left hand.

Memory aid: The initial indicates the word
(except for *denomination*), and the position suggests that the *church* is built on a
solid foundation.

Example: Our *church* has a seminar next
week.

CLEAN, NICE, PURE

Move the palm of the right flat hand
across the palm of the left flat hand from
wrist to fingertips.

Memory aid: Symbolizes the washing of
the hands.

Example: Do you have a *clean* shirt?

CLOSE, SHUT

Bring both flat hands together from the sides with palms facing forward.

Memory aid: Suggests the *closing* of window drapes.

Example: The restaurant is *closed*.

CLOTHES, DRESS, GARMENT, GOWN, SUIT, WEAR

Brush the fingertips of both flat open hands down the chest a few times.

Memory aid: Suggests the smoothing of *clothes* over the body.

Examples: This *dress* is very colorful. I'd like a brown *suit* this time.

COAT, JACKET, OVERCOAT

Move the thumbs of both *A* hands downward from either side of the base of the neck to the center of the lower chest.

Memory aid: The movement follows the lines of *jacket* lapels.

Example: You'll need to wear a *coat* today.

COFFEE

Make a counterclockwise circular movement with the right *S* hand over the left *S* hand.

Memory aid: Symbolizes grinding *coffee* beans by hand.

Example: I drink too much *coffee*.

COLD, CHILLY, FRIGID, WINTER

Hold up both *S* hands in front of the chest and shake them.

Memory aid: Suggests a person shivering in the *cold*.

Example: It's too *cold* to go out.

COLD (sickness)

Place the thumb and bent index finger on either side of the nose and draw down a few times.

Memory aid: Symbolizes wiping the nose.

Example: I had a terrible *cold* last week.

COLOR

Point the fingertips of the open right hand toward the mouth and wiggle them as the hand moves slightly out. Some signers begin this sign by touching the lips with the fingertips.

Memory aid: The fingers can suggest the different *colors* of a rainbow.

Example: What is your favorite *color*?

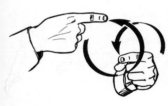

COME

Point both index fingers toward each other and rotate them around each other while simultaneously moving them toward the body. *Note:* See *go. Alternative* (not illustrated): The common action of beckoning with the hand or index finger.

Memory aid: Both signs symbolize the idea of *coming* closer to self.

Example: When will you *come* to see me?

COMPLAIN, COUGH, GRIPE, GRUMBLE, OBJECT, PROTEST

Strike the fingertips of the curved right open hand sharply against the chest. Repeat a few times. When signing *cough* the mouth may be open to simulate the coughing.

Memory aid: Suggests the figurative idea of something on the chest, or in the case of *cough,* violent action in the chest area.

Examples: Joe *complained* bitterly. I need some *cough* medicine.

CONQUER, BEAT, DEFEAT, OVERCOME, SUBDUE

Move the right *S* hand forward and down across the wrist of the left *S* hand.

Memory aid: The right hand dominates the left.

Example: The visiting team was *defeated*.

CONTINUE, ENDURE, LASTING, PERMANENT, PERSEVERE

Place the tip of the right *A* thumb behind the left *A* thumb and move both hands forward together. The palms face down.

Memory aid: Suggests a determination to *continue* forward.

Examples: He received a *lasting* impression. *Persevering* practice will produce results.

COOK (verb), COOK (noun), FRY

Place first the palm side and then the back of the right flat hand on the upturned palm of the left flat hand. *Note:* To sign *cook* as a noun, add the sign for *person* (personalizing word ending).

Memory aid: Suggests the turning over of food in a *frying* pan.

Example: Is the turkey *cooked* yet?

COOKIE, BISCUIT

Place the right *C* thumb and fingertips into the left flat palm and twist. Repeat a few times. *Note:* The sign for *biscuit* makes the right hand raise a few times but not twist.

Memory aid: Suggests using a *cookie* cutter.

Example: Cream-filled *cookies* are a real temptation to me.

COST, CHARGE, EXPENSE, FEE, FINE, PRICE, TAX

Strike the right crooked index finger against the left flat palm with a downward movement.

Memory aid: Suggests the idea of making a dent in one's finances.

Examples: What will it *cost* me? I'll have to pay the *fine*.

COUNTRY (national territory)

Rub the palm side of the right *Y* hand in a counterclockwise direction on the underside of the left forearm near the elbow.

Memory aid: Can suggest a patriotic willingness to wear out one's elbows for one's *country*. The *Y* hand indicates the last letter of the word and is necessary to distinguish it from the sign for *farm*.

Example: The tour covers six *countries*.

CRAZY, NUTS

Point the right curved open hand to the temple and rotate back and forth from the wrist. *Alternative*: Point the right index finger to the temple and make a small circular movement.

Memory aid: Both signs symbolize a scrambled brain.

Example: He has to be *crazy* to attempt that.

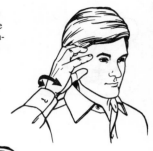

CRY, BAWL, SOB, TEARDROP, TEARS, WEEP

Move one or both index fingers down the cheeks from underneath the eyes a few times.

Memory aid: Suggests falling *tears*.

Examples: She was *bawling*. His eyes were red from *weeping*.

CUP

Put the little-finger edge of the right *C* hand on the left flat palm.

Memory aid: Indicates the size and shape of a *cup*.

Example: Give me a *cup* of coffee.

CUTE

Stroke the chin several times with the fingers of the right *U* hand. Assume a smiling expression.

Memory aid: The sound of *U* rhymes with *cute*.

Example: She's such a *cute* girl.

D

DARK, DIM

Cross the palms of both flat hands down in front of the face.

Memory aid: *Darkness* is created by the eyes being covered.

Example: The room was plunged into *darkness*.

DAUGHTER

First sign *woman*, then move the right flat hand with palm facing up into the crook of the left bent elbow.

Memory aid: Indicates a female baby cradled in the arms.

Example: They have a brilliant *daughter*.

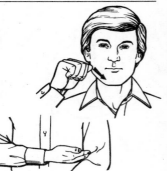

DAY, ALL DAY

Point the left index finger to the right with palm down. Rest the right elbow on the left index finger with the right index finger pointing upward. Move right index finger and arm in a partial arc across the body from right to left. To sign *all day*, hold right index finger as far to the right as possible before beginning to make arc across the body.

Memory aid: The left arm suggests the horizon; right arm the sun's movement.

Examples: On what *day* shall we go? Mark is on duty *all day*.

DEAF

Touch or point to the right ear with the right index finger. Place both downturned flat hands to the front and draw them together until the index fingers and thumbs touch. This last movement is the sign for *closed*.

Memory aid: Suggests that the ears are closed.

Example: I have many *deaf* friends.

DEATH, DEAD, DIE, EXPIRE, PERISH

Hold both flat hands to the front with the right palm facing up and the left palm facing down. Move both hands in an arc to the left while changing the hand positions so that the palms reverse direction.

Memory aid: Symbolizes a body rolling over at the moment of *death*.

Example: The old dog quietly *expired*.

DENTIST

Touch the teeth with the thumb of the right *D* hand.

Memory aid: The initial and location combined suggest the meaning.

Example: When did you last visit a *dentist*?

DIFFER, DISAGREE, CONTRADICT, CONTRARY TO

Touch the forehead with the right index finger; then bring both *D* hands to chest level with palms facing in and index fingertips touching. Move the hands outward sharply in opposite directions. *Note:* When someone is signing rapidly during conversation, the fingertips may not actually touch.

Memory aid: A separating of minds is suggested.

Examples: I have a right to *disagree*. Don't *contradict* me. Their intentions are *contrary to* ours. We can agree to *differ*.

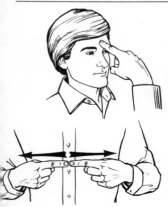

DIFFERENT, DIFFER, DIVERSE, UNLIKE, VARIED

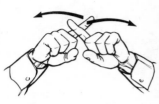

Cross both index fingers with palms facing out; then draw them apart beyond the width of the body. *Note:* Compare *but*.

Memory aid: The movement in opposite directions indicates the meaning.

Example: The two sisters dressed very *differently*.

DIFFICULT, HARD

Strike the knuckles of both bent *V* hands as they are moved up and down.

Memory aid: The striking action makes it more *difficult* for the up-and-down movement.

Example: It is *difficult* to avoid problems with some people.

DINNER, SUPPER

Move the fingers of the right closed *and* hand to the mouth a few times and place the curved right hand over the back of the left flat hand. *Note:* This sign is a combination of *eat* and *night*.

Memory aid: Suggests the meal eaten when the sun has set.

Example: Joyce invited Sally to *dinner*.

DIRTY, FILTHY, FOUL, NASTY

Place the back of the right hand under the chin and wiggle the fingers. *Note*: Compare *pig*.

Memory aid: Like the sign for *pig*.

Example: Your shoes are *filthy*.

DIVORCE

Hold both *D* hands with palms facing and knuckles touching. Twist both hands outward and sideways until the palms face forward. *Alternative* (not illustrated): First sign *marriage*, then move the hands apart with palms facing each other to the *A* position.

Memory aid: Two people once close to each other now separate.

Example: Larry is *divorced*.

DO, ACTION, CONDUCT, DEED, DONE, PERFORM

Point both *C* hands down to the front and move them simultaneously first to one side and then the other.

Memory aid: Suggests being busy with one thing and another.

Examples: He *does* odd jobs. You will *conduct* a survey for us. She *performs* her duties faithfully.

DOCTOR, PHYSICIAN, PSYCHIATRY, SURGEON

Place the right *D* hand or *M* fingers on the upturned left wrist. Use the right *P* hand for *psychiatry*.

Memory aid: Suggests taking a person's pulse rate.

Example: What is your *doctor*'s name?

DOG

Slap the right flat hand against the right leg and snap the right middle finger.

Memory aid: A common gesture for attracting a *dog*'s attention.

Example: Our two *dogs* are brother and sister.

DON'T CARE

Place the fingers of the closed *and* hand on the forehead; then flick the hand forward while simultaneously opening the fingers.

Memory aid: Suggests that the concern of the mind is discarded.

Example: I *don't care* what you do anymore.

DON'T KNOW, DIDN'T RECOGNIZE

Place the fingers of the right flat hand on the forehead (the sign for *know*); then move the right hand away from the forehead with the palm facing forward.

Memory aid: The turning-away action indicates the negative.

Examples: We *don't know* the way home. Jim *didn't recognize* me.

DON'T WANT

Move both open curved hands from a palm-up to a palm-down position.

Memory aid: Suggests throwing something down or away.

Example: He *doesn't want* to go.

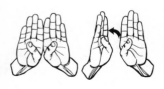

DOOR

Hold both *B* hands to the front with palms facing out and index fingers touching. Twist the right hand back and forth from the wrist.

Memory aid: Symbolizes the opening and closing of a *door*.

Example: Open the *door*.

DOWN

Point the right index finger down with palm facing in, and move it down slightly.

Memory aid: Pointing *downward*.

Example: The pilot looked *down* at the runway.

DRINK

Move the right *C* hand in a short arc toward the mouth.

Memory aid: Suggests the action of *drinking* from a glass.

Example: I love to *drink* orange juice.

DROP

Hold both *S* hands to the front with palms down. Drop them sharply while simultaneously changing to open hands.

Memory aid: Suggests something slipping out of the hands.

Example: Marion decided to *drop* the course. The catcher *dropped* the ball.

E

EACH, EVERY, EVERYBODY, EVERYONE

Hold the left *A* hand to the front with palm facing right. The knuckles and thumb of the right *A* hand rub downward on the left thumb a few times. *Note*: Add the numerical sign for *one* when signing *everyone* and *everybody*.

Memory aid: The right thumb seems to be giving recognition to the left thumb.

Examples: Pete jogs thirty miles *every* week. *Everyone* is invited.

EAR, HEAR, NOISE, SOUND

Touch or point to the right ear with the right index finger. *Note:* Compare *hearing*.

Memory aid: The *ear* is identified by pointing.

Examples: Can you *hear* me? What does that *sound* like?

EAST

Move the right *E* hand to the right with palm facing forward.

Memory aid: The initial and direction of the movement indicate the meaning.

Example: The *eastern* sky was brilliant.

EASY, SIMPLE

Hold the left curved hand to the front with the palm up. Brush the little-finger edge of the right curved hand upward over the fingertips of the left hand several times.

Memory aid: The left fingers are moved *easily*.

Examples: I can *easily* paint my room. This crossword puzzle is *simple*.

EAT, CONSUME, DINE, FOOD, MEAL

The right *and* hand moves toward the mouth a few times.

Memory aid: Putting *food* into the mouth.

Examples: Don't *eat* too much. Where shall we *dine* today?

EGG

Bring the middle finger of the right *H* hand down upon the index finger of the left *H* and move both hands down and out. Most of the latter movement can be done from the wrists.

Memory aid: Suggests the action of removing an *egg* from its shell by breaking the shell.

Example: Some people prefer brown *eggs*.

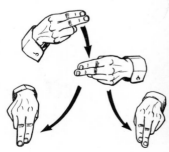

ELECTRICITY, PHYSICS

Strike the bent index and middle fingers of each hand (or just the index fingers) together a few times. The other fingers are closed.

Memory aid: Suggests *electrical* lines being brought together.

Example: Never play with *electricity*.

EMPTY, BARE, NAKED, VACANT

Place the right middle finger on the back of the downturned left hand and move it from the wrist to beyond the knuckles.

Memory aid: Symbolizes the idea that the back of a hand is *empty* and *bare*.

Example: The room was *empty*.

ENEMY, FOE, OPPONENT, RIVAL

Point the two index fingers toward each other with palms facing in. Move them outward sharply in opposite directions; then add the sign for *person* (personalizing word ending).

Memory aid: Symbolizes *enemies* drawing further and further apart.

Examples: He is acting like an *enemy*. John's chess *opponent* is skillful.

EXCITE, AROUSE, STIMULATE, THRILL

Stroke the chest a few times, using both middle fingers alternately with a forward circular motion. Extend the other fingers.

Memory aid: Suggests the heart beating faster in *excitement*.

Examples: I'm *excited* about this new business. Johnny was *thrilled* with his new toy.

EXPLAIN, DEFINE, DESCRIBE

Point the extended fingers of both *F* hands forward with palms facing; then move the hands back and forth alternately. For added clarity the *D* hands may be used for *define* and *describe*.

Memory aid: The action seems to suggest that the hands are not sure which way to go until further *explanation* is given.

Example: Can you *explain* your method to us?

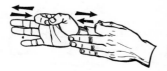

EYE

Point to the eye with the right index finger.

Memory aid: The *eye* is identified by pointing.

Example: I have gray *eyes*.

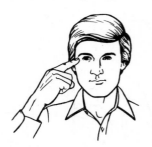

F

FACE

Move the right index finger in a counter-clockwise direction around the face.

Memory aid: The action points to the *face*.

Example: Your *face* is red.

FALL

Stand the right *V* fingers in the left flat palm. Flip them over so that the back of the *V* fingers rests on the left palm.

Memory aid: Symbolizes a person *falling* flat on the back.

Example: Don't *fall* down the steps.

FALL, AUTUMN

Hold the left arm upright with a slight lean to the right. Move the right index-finger side of the right flat hand downward along the left forearm.

Memory aid: Symbolizes the falling of leaves.

Example: The *fall* weather can be quite cold.

FALSE, ARTIFICIAL, COUNTERFEIT, FAKE, PSEUDO, SHAM

Point the right index finger up and move it across the lips from right to left.

Memory aid: Symbolizes the idea that spoken truth is diverted from its normally straight course.

Examples: He has an *artificial* leg. This is *counterfeit* money.

FAMILY

Place both upright *F* hands to the front with the palms facing each other. Make an outward circular movement with each hand simultaneously until the little fingers touch.

Memory aid: The two *F* hands describe the circle of a *family*.

Example: He comes from a respectable *family*.

FAST, IMMEDIATELY, QUICK, RAPID, SPEEDY, SUDDENLY, SWIFT

Flick the right thumb from the crooked index finger.

Memory aid: Suggests the *rapid* flicking of a marble from the hand.

Example: He was driving too *fast*.

FASTING

Move the right thumb and index-side of the *F* hand across the mouth from left to right. *Note:* Compare *dry*.

Memory aid: The initial indicates the word, and the action suggests dryness of the mouth.

Example: The doctor prescribed a three-day *fast* from solid food.

FAT, CHUBBY, OBESE, PLUMP, STOUT

Place both curved open hands by the cheeks and move outward.

Memory aid: Suggests the large round cheeks of a *fat* person.

Example: Too much starchy food will make you *fat*.

FATHER

Considered informal but commonly used is the sign made by touching the forehead with the thumb of the right open hand. The fingers may be wiggled slightly. *Alternative* (not illustrated): First sign *male*; then follow by moving the right hand to the left with palm up.

Memory aid: Indicates the head male of the family unit.

Example: His *father* is coming soon.

FAVORITE, LUCKY

Tap the chin a few times with the right middle finger. To sign *lucky*, touch the chin with the right middle finger; then flip the hand around so that the palm faces forward.

Memory aid: Suggests a dimple on the chin, which is considered cute by many people.

Example: She baked my *favorite* pie.

FEELING, MOTIVE, SENSATION

Move the right middle finger upward on the chest with other fingers extended.

Memory aid: Suggests the direction of inner *feelings*.

Examples: How do you *feel*? My *motive* is right.

FEET

Point first to one foot and then the other.

Memory aid: Both *feet* are identified by pointing to them.

Example: My *feet* are tired.

FINE

Place the thumb edge of the right flat open hand at the chest and pivot the hand forward. *Note:* Compare *polite*.

Memory aid: Symbolizes an old-fashioned shirt or blouse with ruffles.

Example: I'm just *fine* today.

FINGERSPELLING, ALPHABET, DACTYLOLOGY, MANUAL ALPHABET, SPELL

With palm facing down, wiggle the fingers of the right flat open hand as the hand moves along a horizontal line to the right.

Memory aid: Emphasizes the use of fingers in *fingerspelling*.

Examples: I can only communicate with the *manual alphabet*. Advanced *dactylology* takes a lot of practice.

FINISH, ALREADY

Hold both open hands to the front with
palms facing self and fingers pointing up.
Shake them quickly outward to the sides a
few times. *Note*: This sign is used fre-
quently in everyday conversation. For example: Instead of signing, "I've already
been to the store," the deaf person may
simply sign, "Store *finished*."

Memory aid: Symbolizes something being
shaken off by the hands.

Example: I have *finished* my college education.

FIRE, BURN, FLAME, HELL

With palms facing in, move both slightly
curved open hands up and down alternately in front of the body while wiggling
the fingers. When signing *hell*, the right
index finger can be pointed down as an addition.

Memory aid: Symbolizes leaping *flames*.

Example: Don't *burn* yourself with that
match.

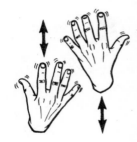

FISH (noun)

Place the fingertips of the left flat hand at
the right wrist or elbow. Point the right
flat hand forward with palm facing left,
and swing from right to left a few times.
Most of the movement is at the wrist.

Memory aid: Suggests the swimming motion of a *fish*'s tail.

Example: There are plenty of *fish* in this
pond.

FLOWER

Place the fingertips of the right *and* hand under each nostril separately.

Memory aid: Suggests smelling a *flower*.

Example: Janet was thrilled with the bouquet of *flowers*.

FOOLISH, NONSENSE, RIDICULOUS, SILLY

Pass the right *Y* hand rapidly back and forth in front of the forehead a few times. The palm faces left.

Memory aid: Suggests a young or childish mind that constantly fluctuates in opinion.

Examples: How could you be so *foolish*? That is *nonsense* to me.

FOOTBALL

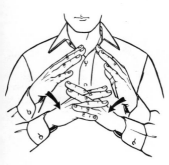

Interlock the fingers of both hands vigorously a few times.

Memory aid: Suggests the strong physical contact made in *football*.

Example: When is the next *football* game?

FOR

Touch the right temple with the right index finger; then dip it straight forward until the index finger is pointing forward.

Memory aid: Knowledge is directed outward *for* a particular purpose.

Example: What can you do *for* me?

FORGET, FORSAKE

Wipe the palm side of the right open hand across the forehead from left to right. End with the right hand in the *A* position close to the right temple.

Memory aid: Indicates wiping information from the mind.

Examples: I will not *forget* you.

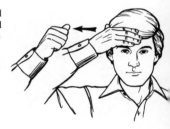

FORK

Move the fingers of the right *V* hand into the left upturned palm a few times. *Note:* Sometimes the three fingers of the right *M* hand are used.

Memory aid: The fingers symbolize the tines of a *fork*.

Example: I would rather use a *fork*.

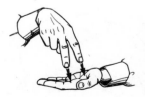

FRENCH FRIES

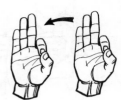

Sign the right *F* hand once, then again a second time slightly to the right.

Memory aid: The two initials are used.

Example: Homemade *french fries* are delicious.

FRIDAY

Make a small clockwise circle with the right *F* hand.

Memory aid: The initial suggests the word, and the circular motion suggests the passing of time.

Example: Come on *Friday*.

FRIEND, FRIENDSHIP

Interlock the right and left index fingers and repeat in reverse.

Memory aid: Suggests the link of *friendship*.

Example: We've been *friends* over twenty years.

FRIGHTENED, AFRAID, SCARED, TERRIFIED

Move both *and* hands simultaneously across the chest from the sides in opposite directions. During the movement, change the hand positions to open hands.

Memory aid: Suggests the reaction of self-protection.

Examples: He was *scared* by the movie. Being alone in the dark *terrified* her.

FROM

Touch the upright left index finger with the knuckle of the right *X* index finger; then move the right hand in a slight backward-downward arc. *Note:* Sometimes the left index finger is crooked or pointed forward.

Memory aid: Suggests pulling back *from* something.

Example: I'm leaving *from* the bus terminal.

FRUIT

Place the thumb and index fingers of the right *F* hand on the right cheek. Twist forward or backward. *Alternative* (not illustrated): Make the sign for *grow*; then place the right curved open hand over the left *and* hand. Slide the right fingers off the left hand to the right until the right hand also forms an *and* hand.

Memory aid: The basic sign is similar to the one for *apple*. The alternative sign suggests the growth and shape of *fruit*.

Example: Fruit is excellent for one's health.

FUN, AMUSING, COMICAL, FUNNY, HILARIOUS, HUMOROUS

Brush the tip of the nose with the fingers of the right *U* hand. Move the right *U* hand down and brush the left and right *U* fingers up and down against each other a few times. *Note:* Sign *amusing, comical, funny, hilarious,* and *humorous* by brushing the nose several times only.

Memory aid: Suggests that people's noses wrinkle when they laugh.

Examples: Skating is *fun*. That man is *funny*.

FUTURE, LATER ON, BY AND BY, SOMEDAY

Hold the right flat hand with palm facing left in an upright position close to the right temple. Move it in a forward-upward arc. The greater the arc, the more distant the future that is indicated.

Memory aid: Suggests moving onward into the *future*.

Examples: You have an exciting *future*. Pamela will know more *later on*. The truth will come out *someday*.

G

GAME, CHALLENGE

Hold both *A* hands in front and to the sides of the chest with palms facing self. Bring the hands firmly together until the knuckles touch.

Memory aid: Suggests that the hands are competing with each other.

Example: Sam loves a *game* of chess.

GASOLINE

Bring the right *A* thumb down into the left *O* hand.

Memory aid: Symbolizes putting *gas* into an automobile tank.

Example: You're almost out of *gas*.

GET, ACQUIRE, OBTAIN, RECEIVE

Bring both open hands together while simultaneously forming *S* hands and place the right on top of the left. The hands can be moved toward the body, especially when signing *receive*.

Memory aid: Suggests taking hold of something and drawing it to oneself.

Example: He *received* the award graciously.

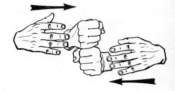

GIFT, AWARD, BESTOW, CONFER, CONTRIBUTE, PRESENT, REWARD

With the palms facing each other, place both closed hands to the front with the thumb tips touching the inside of their respective crooked index fingers. Move both hands forward simultaneously in an arc.

Memory aid: A natural gesture of *giving* something to someone.

Examples: Please accept this small *gift*. I'd like to make a *contribution*.

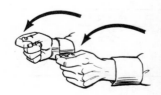

GIRL, MAIDEN

First sign *woman;* then move the right flat hand to waist level with palm facing down to indicate the height of a girl.

Memory aid: Indicates a *girl's* height.

Example: That *girl* is tall.

GIVE, DISTRIBUTE

Hold both *and* hands to the front with palms facing down. Move them forward simultaneously while forming flat hands with fingers pointing forward and palms facing up.

Memory aid: Suggests the act of *giving*.

Example: I want to *give* you a present.

GO

Point both index fingers toward each other and rotate them around each other as they are moved away from the body.

Memory aid: Symbolizes moving away from the present location.

Example: I'll *go* tomorrow.

GOD

Point the right *G* finger in a forward-upward direction at head level. (Some signers use the whole flat hand with the palm facing left.) Move the right hand in a backward-downward arc toward self, ending with a *B* hand in front of the upper chest with palm still facing left.

Memory aid: The finger or hand pointing upward suggests *God* is above all. The *B* hand in the position for *be* can suggest the eternal existence of *God*.

Example: *God* is omniscient.

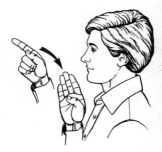

GONE, ABSENT

Draw the right open hand down through the left *C* hand and end with the right hand in the *and* position below the left hand.

Memory aid: Suggests something disappearing down a hole.

Example: My money is *gone*.

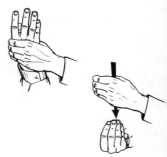

GOOD, WELL

Place the fingers of the right flat hand at the lips; then move the hand down into the palm of the left hand with both palms facing up. *Alternative* (not illustrated): Raise the right thumb in the "thumbs up" position for informal use.

Memory aid: Suggests something that has been tasted, approved, and offered to another.

Example: We have found their merchandise to be of *good* quality.

GRANDFATHER

Touch the forehead with the thumb of the right open hand which has its palm facing left. Move the right hand in two forward arcs. *Alternative* (not illustrated): Begin with the informal sign for *father*; then hold both open hands to the front with palms up and move twice toward the left shoulder.

Memory aid: The combination of the sign for *father* and the double hand movements of both signs suggest the reference to someone of the older generation.

Example: My *grandfather* is ninety.

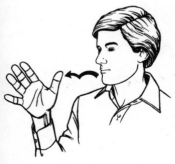

GRANDMOTHER

Touch the chin with the thumb of the right open hand which has its palm facing left. Move the right hand in two forward arcs. *Alternative* (not illustrated): Begin with the informal sign for *mother*; then hold both open hands to the front with palms up and move twice toward the left shoulder.

Memory aid: The combination of the sign for *mother* and the double hand movements of both signs suggest the reference to someone of the older generation.

Example: We will see *Grandmother* today.

GREEN

Hold the right *G* hand to the right while shaking it from the wrist.

Memory aid: The initial indicates the word, which requires context and simultaneous lipreading for full comprehension.

Example: My grass is not very *green*.

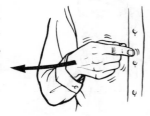

GUESS, MISS (let slip or let go)

The same basic sign is used for both words. Move the right *C* hand across the face from right to left and close to a down-turned *S* position.

Memory aid: Suggests an attempt to catch something in midair.

Examples: Can you *guess* my age? I'm afraid I *missed* my appointment.

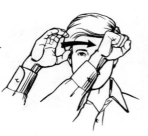

HALF

H

Cross the right index finger over the left index finger and pull it back toward self. *Alternative:* Pull the little-finger edge of the right flat hand toward self across the left flat hand.

Memory aid: Suggests *half* of a finger or *half* of a hand.

Example: Please give me my *half*.

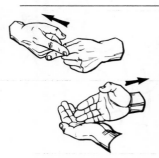

HAMBURGER

Cup the right hand on top of the left cupped hand; then reverse.

Memory aid: Suggests the shaping of *hamburger* patties.

Example: I prefer my *hamburgers* without mustard.

HANDS

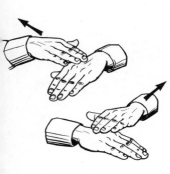

Place the downturned right hand over the back of the downturned left hand. Move the right hand toward self, and repeat the action with the left hand over the right.

Memory aid: Each *hand* is referred to individually without reference to the arm.

Example: He washed his *hands* in the sink.

HAPPEN, EVENT, OCCUR

Point both index fingers up with palms facing. Pivot both hands forward from the wrists so that the palms face forward.

Memory aid: Two pointing hands suggest the importance of noticing something.

Example: What *happened* to Nancy's car?

HAPPY, DELIGHT, GLAD, JOY, MERRY

Move both flat hands in forward circular movements with palms touching the chest alternately or simultaneously. One hand is often used by itself.

Memory aid: Suggests *happy* feelings springing up from within.

Examples: I'm very *happy* for you. You must be *delighted*.

HARD-OF-HEARING

Point the right *H* hand forward and move it in a short arc to the right.

Memory aid: The use of two *H* positions suggests the phrase.

Example: My uncle is *hard-of-hearing*.

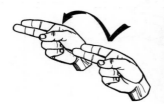

HATE, ABHOR, DESPISE, DETEST, LOATHE

Hold both open hands in front of the chest with palms facing down, and flick both middle fingers outward simultaneously.

Memory aid: Symbolizes the desire to get rid of something.

Examples: I *hate* mathematics. Corine *loathes* insects of all kinds.

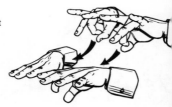

HAVE, HAS, HAD, OWN, POSSESS

Place the fingertips of both bent hands on the chest.

Memory aid: Symbolizes pointing out personal *ownership*.

Examples: Kevin *has* measles. We *possess* two cars.

HE, HIM

First sign *man;* then point the index finger forward. If it is obvious that a male is being referred to, the sign for *man* can be omitted.

Memory aid: The signer directs attention by pointing.

Examples: He is a studious person. Please give *him* the book.

HEALTHY, ROBUST, WELL, WHOLESOME

Place the fingertips and thumbs of both curved open hands on the chest, then move them forward while forming *S* hands. *Note:* Compare *strong*.

Memory aid: Suggests that the body has strength.

Examples: I'm thankful for a *healthy* family. I feel *well* now.

HEARING

Place the right index finger in front of the mouth and make a few small forward circular movements. *Note:* Compare *say*.

Memory aid: The sign is similar to the one for *say* and indicates that a *hearing* person can learn to speak easily.

Example: Is your friend a *hearing* person or deaf?

HEARING AID

Place the curved fingers of the right *V* hand at the right ear. Twist a few times.

Memory aid: Suggests placing a *hearing aid* in the ear.

Example: His *hearing aid* was impossible to see.

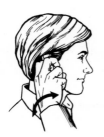

HEART (physical)

Place the right middle finger over the heart with the other fingers extended.

Memory aid: The right hand feels for a heartbeat.

Example: He ran until his *heart* was beating rapidly.

HELP, AID, ASSIST, BOOST

Place the closed right hand on the flat left palm and lift both hands together.

Memory aid: Suggests the giving of a *helping* hand.

Examples: His *aid* was appreciated. Their donation was a real *boost* to the fund.

HERE

Hold both flat hands to the front with palms facing up. Make forward semicircles in opposite directions.

Memory aid: A natural gesture.

Example: It happened *here*.

HI, HELLO

Place the right flat hand to the right temple area of the head with the palm facing forward. Move the hand a short distance forward and to the right.

Memory aid: Reminds one of a military salute.

Example: Hi, my name is Richard.

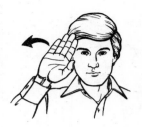

HIS, HER, YOUR, THEIR

Push the right flat hand forward with palm facing out toward the person or persons being referred to. The signs for *male* and *female* can precede *his* and *her* if it is not obvious from the context. Add a final move to the right when using *your* in the plural.

Memory aid: Suggests the idea of something separate or apart from the signer.

Examples: His desk is cluttered. Have you visited *their* home?

HOME

Place the fingertips of the right *and* hand first at the mouth, then at the right cheek. Sometimes the position at the cheek is made with a slightly curved hand.

Memory aid: Suggests the place where one eats and sleeps.

Example: I'm going *home* tomorrow.

HORSE

Extend the thumb of the right *U* hand and place it on the right temple with palm facing forward. Bend and unbend the *U* fingers a few times.

Memory aid: Suggests the movement of a *horse*'s ears.

Example: Melanie wants a *horse* of her own.

HOSPITAL, PATIENT

Use the right *H* or *P* fingers for *hospital* and *patient* respectively, and draw a cross on the upper left arm.

Memory aid: Symbolizes the Red Cross emblem for the relief of suffering.

Example: Mike is a *patient* at St. Luke's Hospital.

HOT

Place the fingers and thumb of the right *C* hand at the sides of the mouth, then quickly pivot the hand forward to the right.

Memory aid: Suggests removing *hot* food from the mouth.

Example: It's too *hot* to work.

HOUR

Point the fingers of the left flat hand either
up or forward with palm facing right.
Move the index finger of the right *D* hand
in a complete clockwise circle by rotating
the wrist. Keep the right index finger in
constant contact with the left hand.

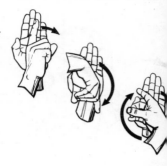

Memory aid: Follows the movement of a
minute hand on a clock.

Example: I will be gone for one *hour*.

HOW

Point the fingers of both bent hands down
and place the hands back to back. Revolve
the hands in and upward together until the
palms are flat and facing up.

Memory aid: The appearance of the palms
suggests the idea of showing *how*.

Example: How are you doing today?

HUNGER, APPETITE, CRAVE, FAMINE, STARVE

Move the thumb and fingers of the right *C*
hand down the center of the chest from
just below the throat. *Note:* Compare
wish.

Memory aid: Suggests the direction that
food travels to the stomach.

Examples: I'm *hungry*. He has an enormous *appetite*.

HURRY, HUSTLE, RUSH

Move one or both *H* hands quickly forward in short arcs. *Note:* If two hands are used, they can be quickly raised up and down alternately.

Memory aid: Suggests someone walking rapidly.

Examples: What's your *hurry*? It's a *rush* job.

HUSBAND

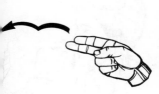

First sign *man;* then clasp the hands with the right hand above the left. The latter position is the sign for *marriage.*

Memory aid: Indicates a married male.

Example: She has a handsome *husband.*

I

Position the right *I* hand with palm facing left and thumb touching the chest.

Memory aid: The initial *I* in close proximity to the body suggests the individual.

Example: Do you know what *I* want?

ICE CREAM, LOLLIPOP

Pull the right *S* hand toward the mouth with a downward twist a few times. The tongue may also be shown.

Memory aid: The action of licking an *ice cream* cone.

Example: Paul dropped his *ice cream* on the ground.

IF

Point the two *F* hands forward and move them up and down alternately with palms facing each other.

Memory aid: The movement suggests scales that may tip one way or the other.

Example: *If* you go, I will also.

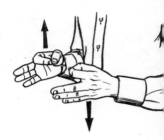

IMPORTANT, MERIT, PRECIOUS, SIGNIFICANT, USEFUL, VALUABLE, WORTHY

Bring both *F* hands up to the center of the chest and turn them palms down with the thumbs and index fingers touching. *Note:* Compare *worthless*.

Memory aid: The *F* hands can represent something that is first and, therefore, *important*.

Example: She has an *important* responsibility.

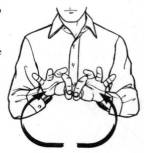

IMPROVE

Move the little-finger edge of the right flat hand in small arcs up the left arm.

Memory aid: Suggests degrees of *improvement*.

Example: Donna's piano playing is *improving*.

IN, INTO, ENTER

Move the closed fingers of the right hand into the left *C* hand. *Note:* To sign *into* and *enter*, the right fingers can be pushed down right through the left *C* hand.

Memory aid: Symbolizes going *into* a hole.

Examples: Is it safe to go *into* that building? Why did she *enter* college so late?

INTEREST

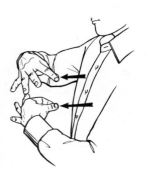

Place the thumb and index finger of each hand on the chest, with one hand above the other. Bring the index fingers and thumbs together as the hands are moved forward. Keep the other fingers extended.

Memory aid: Suggests that a person's inner feelings are being drawn toward something.

Example: I found our conversation *interesting*.

INTERPRET, REVERSE
INTERPRET, TRANSLATE

Hold the *F* hands with palms facing and
the left palm facing forward; then rotate
positions so that the right palm faces forward. To sign *reverse interpret*, use the *R*
hands with the reverse action of *interpret*,
and follow with the regular sign for *interpret*. To sign *translate*, use *T* hands and
make the same movement as for *interpret*.

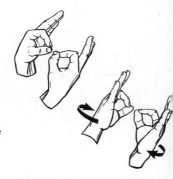

Memory aid: The changing positions of the
hands suggest the idea of changing from
one language to another.

Example: Will you *interpret* for me?

JEALOUS

J

Put the right little fingertip at the corner
of the mouth and give it a twist.

Memory aid: The little finger suggests the
J, which causes the mouth to open and
drool with *jealousy*.

Example: They both suffer from *jealousy*.

KEEP, CARE, CAREFUL,
SUPERVISE

K

Cross the wrist of the right *V* hand over
the wrist of the left *V* hand. To sign *careful*, the right wrist should strike the left
wrist a few times. To sign *care* and *supervise*, move both hands in a counterclockwise circle in the *keep* position.

Memory aid: The fingers can symbolize
four watchful eyes.

Examples: Please *keep* a *careful* watch on
the house. I *supervise* two hundred men.

KID

Extend the index and small finger of the right hand. With the palm facing down, put the index finger under the nose. The hand is then pivoted up and down slightly and often moved to the right simultaneously.

Memory aid: Suggests the running nose of a young child.

Example: Beverly took her *kids* to the pool today.

KISS

Place the fingers of the right hand on the lips and then on the cheek.

Memory aid: Suggests two common locations for *kissing*.

Example: They *kissed* when they met.

KITCHEN

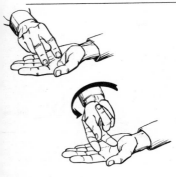

Place the right *K* hand first palm down, then palm up on the upturned left palm.

Memory aid: The action suggests food being turned over in a pan.

Example: You have a beautiful *kitchen*.

KNIFE

Move the right *H* (or index) fingers downward across the left *H* (or index) fingers
several times. *Alternative* (not illustrated):
Move the right index finger back and forth
over the left index finger.

Memory aid: The basic sign symbolizes an
action similar to sharpening a pencil by
hand, while the alternative sign suggests
cutting by its action.

Example: This *knife* needs sharpening.

KNOW, RECOGNIZE, INTELLIGENCE, KNOWLEDGE

Tap the fingers of the right slightly curved
hand on the forehead a few times. *Note:*
Compare *don't know.*

Memory aid: The repository of *knowledge*
is considered to be the brain.

Examples: Do you *know* her? Yes, I *recognize* her. Jane does not possess sufficient
knowledge.

LANGUAGE, TONGUE

L

Point both *L* hands toward each other
(sometimes the index fingers point up),
and move them to the sides with a twisting
motion from the wrists.

Memory aid: The *L* hands indicate the
word, and the action is similar to that of
the sign for *sentence.*

Example: What is your mother *tongue?*

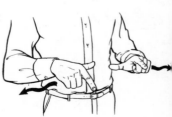

LARGE, BIG, ENORMOUS, GREAT, HUGE, IMMENSE

Hold both *L* hands to the front with palms facing. Move them outward to the sides beyond the width of the body.

Memory aid: The initial and the distance placed between the hands indicate the meaning.

Example: He was carrying an *enormous* box.

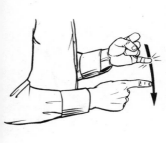

LAST, END, FINAL, LASTLY

Hold the left hand to the front with palm facing self and little finger extended. Strike the left little finger with the right index finger as the right hand moves down. Sometimes this sign is made with both little fingers.

Memory aid: The little finger is considered the *last* finger.

Examples: This is my *last* chance. *Lastly*, I thank all of you sincerely.

LATER, SUBSEQUENTLY, AFTER A WHILE, AFTERWARD, LUTHERAN

Hold the left flat hand up with the palm facing right. Place the thumb of the right *L* in the center of the left palm, and pivot the right index finger forward and down. *Note:* Omit the pivoting movement when signing *Lutheran*.

Memory aid: Suggests the hand of a clock moving an undesignated distance.

Examples: I'll see you *later*. I left the office *after a while*. *Subsequently*, I changed my mind.

LAUGH, CHUCKLE, GIGGLE

Starting near the corners of the mouth, move both index fingers upward over the cheeks a few times. Assume an appropriate facial expression. *Note:* Compare *smile*.

Memory aid: Suggests the upturned mouth.

Examples: We've never *laughed* so much. Sue *chuckled* at the thought.

LAZY, SLOTHFUL

Tap the palm of the right *L* hand at the left shoulder several times.

Memory aid: Suggests that a person needs to shoulder his or her load of the work.

Example: He's the *laziest* individual I know.

LEARN, STUDENT

Place the fingers of the right open hand on the upturned left palm. Close the right fingers as the hand is moved to the forehead. The fingertips are then placed on the forehead. To sign *student,* add the sign for *person* (personalizing word ending).

Memory aid: The right hand seems to be taking information from the left hand and putting it into the mind. The left hand can represent a book.

Example: How can you *learn* with all this noise?

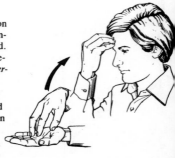

LEAVE, DEPART, RETIRE, WITHDRAW

Bring both flat hands up from the right and close to *A* hands.

Memory aid: The hands *leave* one position for another.

Example: What time are you *leaving*?

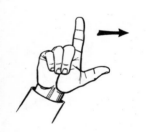

LEFT (direction)

Move the right *L* hand toward the left.

Memory aid: The initial and direction indicate the meaning.

Example: Turn first *left*, then right.

LETTER, MAIL

Place the right *A* thumb on the mouth and then on the palm of the upturned left hand. *Note:* Compare *stamp*.

Memory aid: Suggests moistening a stamp and placing it on an envelope.

Example: I need a stamp for this *letter*.

LIBRARY

Make a small clockwise circle with the right *L* hand.

Memory aid: The initial indicates the word, which requires context and simultaneous lipreading for full comprehension.

Example: Jennifer's interest in *libraries* began at an early age.

LIE, FALSEHOOD

Point the right index finger to the left and move it horizontally across the lips from right to left.

Memory aid: Symbolizes the idea that spoken truth is diverted from its normally straight course.

Example: Don't *lie* to me.

LIFE, EXISTENCE

Put palm sides of both flat open hands on the abdomen and raise them up to the chest while wiggling fingers. *Existence* may be signed with *E* hands. *Note:* Compare *live*. *Alternative* (not illustrated): Perform the same movement with *L* hands.

Memory aid: The first sign suggests that where there is movement there is *life*, and the second suggests the same with the additional indication of initials.

Example: My *life* is exciting.

LIGHT, BRIGHT, CLEAR, LUMINOUS, OBVIOUS

Hold both *and* hands at chest level with palms down. Open the hands as they are moved up and to the sides with palms facing forward.

Memory aid: Suggests sunbeams shining over the horizon.

Example: The sky was *bright* with morning sunlight.

LIKE, ADMIRE

Place the right thumb and index finger against the chest, with the other fingers extended. Bring the thumb and index finger together as the hand is moved a short distance forward. *Note:* Compare *please*.

Memory aid: Symbolizes the inner feelings going out to someone or something.

Examples: I *admire* his artistic ability. I *like* pears.

LIPREADING, ORAL, SPEECH-READING

Hold the right curved *V* fingers at the mouth. Move around the mouth in a counterclockwise direction.

Memory aid: The initial indicates the voice, and the movement draws attention to the movement of the lips when using the voice.

Example: How good are you at *lipreading*?

LIVE, ADDRESS, DWELL, RESIDE

Move the palm sides of both *L* (or *A*) hands up from the abdomen to the chest. *Note:* Compare *life*.

Memory aid: The initials indicate the word, and the action suggests that just as life *lives* within the body, so the body *resides* at a particular address.

Example: Where do you *live*?

LONG

Extend the left flat hand to the front with palm facing down. Run the right index finger up the left arm, beginning at the fingertips.

Memory aid: Suggests the length of the arm.

Example: He read a *long* poem.

LOOK, LOOK AT, LOOK AT ME, LOOK BACK, LOOK DOWN, GAZE, OBSERVE, WATCH

Point the fingers of the right *V* hand at the eyes and then in the particular direction desired. *Note:* Compare *see*.

Memory aid: The two fingers represent the two eyes.

Example: Look carefully while you drive.

LOSE, LOST

Hold the fingertips of both palm-up *and* hands together; then separate the hands by dropping them down and opening them.

Memory aid: Suggests that something has dropped out of the hands.

Example: I've *lost* one of my gloves.

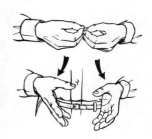

LOUSY, ROTTEN

Place the thumb of the right *3* hand on the nose, then pivot the hand sharply downward. Assume an appropriate facial expression.

Memory aid: Can suggest a person suffering from a head cold with a streaming nose.

Example: This is a *lousy* job.

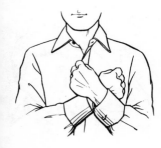

LOVE

Cross either the closed or flat hands over the heart with palms facing in.

Memory aid: Symbolizes the *love* of the heart.

Example: He *loved* her dearly.

LUNCH

Move the fingers of the right closed *and* hand to the mouth a few times. Place the left flat hand at the outer bend of the right elbow, and raise the right forearm to an upright position with palm facing left. *Note:* This sign is a combination of *eat* and *noon*.

Memory aid: Suggests the meal eaten when the sun is overhead.

Example: She cooked *lunch* for us.

MAKE, FASHION, FIX

M

Strike the right *S* hand on the top of the left *S* hand and twist the hands slightly inward. Repeat for emphasis as needed.

Memory aid: Suggests the action of unscrewing something.

Examples: Mother *fixed* a fine meal. He *fashioned* the sculpture with great care.

MAN, MALE

Move the right hand to the forehead as though gripping the peak of a cap between the fingers and thumb; then move it forward a short distance. Some signers add the action of moving the right flat hand forward at head level with the palm facing down when signing *man*.

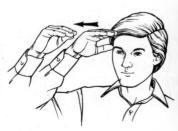

Memory aid: Suggests the old-fashioned tipping of caps and hats by men when greeting others, especially women.

Examples: He is a good *man*. The *male* peacocks are beautiful.

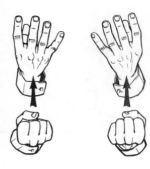

MANY, LOTS, NUMEROUS, PLURAL, SCORES

Hold both *S* hands to the front with palms facing up. Flick the fingers and thumbs open several times.

Memory aid: The use of all the fingers represents the meaning.

Examples: Many people came. He presented *numerous* ideas. His company finances a *plurality* of enterprises.

MARRIAGE

Clasp the hands in a natural position with the right hand above the left.

Memory aid: A couple joins hands during their wedding ceremony.

Examples: They will be *married* in three weeks. Their *marriage* is successful.

MATHEMATICS, ALGEBRA, CALCULUS, GEOMETRY, STATISTICS, TRIGONOMETRY

Make an upward and inward motion with both *M* hands so that the right *M* hand crosses inside the left. Use *A* hands for *algebra,* *C* hands for *calculus,* and so on.

Memory aid: The X-shape movement suggests the multiplication symbol.

Example: Christine made good grades in *algebra.*

MAY, MAYBE, PERHAPS, POSSIBLY, PROBABLY

Hold both flat hands to the front and move them up and down alternately.

Memory aid: Symbolizes the weighing of one thing against another.

Example: Maybe I should go. *Perhaps* she should resign.

ME

Point the right index finger toward the chest.

Memory aid: The signer directs attention to himself.

Example: Can you understand *me*?

MEAT, BEEF, FLESH

Using the right thumb and index finger, pinch the flesh of the left flat hand between the thumb and index finger. *Note: Flesh* can also be signed by using the sign for *body*.

Memory aid: A *fleshy* part of the hand is indicated.

Example: What type of *meat* do you prefer?

MEET, ENCOUNTER

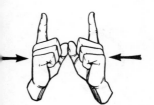

Bring both *D* hands together from the sides with palms facing.

Memory aid: Suggests two persons *meeting*.

Example: I *met* Ruth only yesterday.

MILK

Squeeze one or both slightly open *S* hands with a downward motion. Do it alternately if two hands are used.

Memory aid: Symbolizes the act of *milking* a cow.

Example: I'd like some cold *milk*, please.

MINUTE, MOMENT, SECOND

Hold the flat left hand vertically with palm facing right. Let the index finger of the right *D* hand touch the left palm with the index finger pointing up. Make a short movement forward with the right index finger.

Memory aid: Follows the movement of a *minute* hand on a clock.

Examples: I will be one *minute*. Please wait a *moment*.

MONDAY

Make a small clockwise circle with the
right *M* hand.

Memory aid: The initial suggests the word,
and the circular motion suggests the passing of time.

Example: Come on *Monday.*

MONEY, CAPITAL, FINANCES, FUNDS

Strike the back of the right *and* hand into
the left upturned palm a few times.

Memory aid: Suggests a person showing
another how much *money* is in the hand.

Examples: The project requires a lot of
money. Do you have the *capital*?

MONTH, MONTHLY

Point the left index finger up with palm
facing right. Move the right index finger
from the top to the base of the left index
finger. Repeat a few times to sign
monthly.

Memory aid: The left index finger's three
joints and tip represent the four weeks of
a *month.*

Examples: The project will take two
months. Have you continued with your
monthly report?

MY, MINE, OWN, PERSONAL

Place the palm of the right flat hand on the chest.

Memory aid: The hand over the heart suggests protection of *personal* belongings.

Examples: This is *my* book. Voting is a *personal* right I exercise.

MYSELF, SELF

Bring the *A* hand against the center of the chest with palm facing left.

Memory aid: The thumb can be thought of as representing *self*.

Example: I bought *myself* a present today.

N

NAME, CALLED, NAMED

Cross the middle-finger edge of the right *H* fingers over the index-finger edge of the left *H* fingers. To sign *called* or *named*, move the crossed *H* hands in a small forward arc together.

Memory aid: Reminds one that those who cannot write have to sign their *name* with an *X*.

Example: Please spell your *name* for me.

NEAR, ADJACENT, BY, CLOSE TO

Hold the left curved hand away from the body with palm facing in. Move the back of the right curved hand from a position close to the body to one near the palm of the left hand.

Memory aid: The proximity of the hands suggests the meaning.

Example: The dog obediently came *near*.

NEVER

Trace a half circle in the air to the right with the right flat hand; then drop the hand away to the right.

Memory aid: Suggests a circle that can *never* be completed because the hand has dropped away.

Example: I'll *never* shop there again.

NEW

Pass the back of the slightly curved right hand across the left flat palm from fingers to heel. Continue the movement of the right hand in a slight upward direction.

Memory aid: The right hand seems to be suggesting a *new* direction to the left hand.

Example: Her *new* dress is pretty.

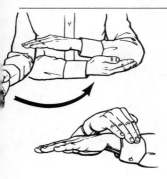

NIGHT, ALL NIGHT

Hold the left arm in a horizontal position with the fingers of the left downturned flat hand pointing right. Place the right forearm on the back of the left hand and point the right curved hand downward. To sign *all night*, make a downward sweeping motion from right to left with the right hand.

Memory aid: The right hand symbolizes the sun going below the horizon.

Example: It's a rainy *night*.

NO

Bring the right thumb, index and middle fingers together.

Memory aid: Suggests a combination of the signs for *N* and *O*.

Example: My answer is *no*.

NONE, NO, NOTHING

Hold both *O* hands in front of the chest and move them to the side in opposite directions. To sign *nothing*, the hands should be open while moving out to the side.

Memory aid: A double zero emphasizes the meaning.

Examples: There is *none* left. We carry *no* spare parts for that model. The fisherman caught *nothing*.

NOON, MIDDAY

Point the left flat hand to the right with palm facing down. Rest the right elbow on the back of the left hand with the right arm in a vertical position and the palm facing left.

Memory aid: The left arm indicates the horizon, and the right hand symbolizes the position of the sun at *midday*.

Example: Lunch will be at *noon*.

NORTH

Move the *N* hand upward.

Memory aid: Indicates the direction on a compass.

Example: The *north* wind is blowing.

NOT, DO NOT

Place the right *A* thumb under the chin and move it forward and away from the chin. *Alternative* (not illustrated): Cross both flat hands with palms down; then uncross them by moving both hands out sideways. The head can also be shaken to emphasize the negative.

Memory aid: The thumb moving out from under the chin suggests something that cannot be swallowed. The uncrossing of the hands is a natural negative sign.

Example: I'll *not* be a part of it.

NOW, CURRENT, IMMEDIATE, PRESENT

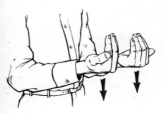

Hold both bent (or *Y*) hands to the front at waist level with palms facing up. Drop both hands sharply a short distance.

Memory aid: Suggests that the hands feel the weight of something *now*.

Examples: Do it *now*. It is a *current* problem. My pain was *immediate*. I predict the *present* situation will not last long.

OLD, AGE, ANCIENT, ANTIQUE

Close the right hand just below the chin and move it downward.

Memory aid: Suggests the beard of an *old* man.

Example: He's as *ancient* as the hills.

ON, OFF

With both palms facing down, place the right flat hand on the back of the left flat hand. To sign *off* add the motion of lifting the right flat hand upward and to the right.

Memory aid: Indicates something *on* top of something else.

Example: The typewriter is *on* the desk.

OPEN

Place the thumbs and index fingers of both flat hands together with the palms facing forward. (Some prefer the palms facing down.) Move both hands sideways in opposite directions.

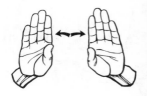

Memory aid: Suggests *opening* drapes.

Example: What time does the store *open*?

ORANGE (color and fruit)

Slightly open and squeeze the right *S* hand in front of the mouth a few times. *Alternative* (not illustrated): The color *orange* can also be signed by holding up the right *O* hand and shaking it from the wrist.

Memory aid: Suggests squeezing an *orange* to obtain the juice.

Example: Would you like an *orange*?

OUR

Place the slightly cupped right hand on the right side of the chest with palm facing left. Move the right hand forward in a circular motion, bringing it to rest near the left shoulder with the palm facing right.

Memory aid: The circular movement suggests the inclusion of others.

Example: Our team is winning.

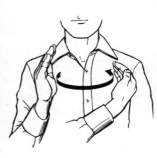

OURSELVES

This sign is a combination of *our* and *self*. *Our* is signed by placing the slightly cupped right hand on the right side of the chest with the palm facing left. Move the right hand forward in a circular motion, bringing it to rest near the left shoulder with the palm facing right. *Self* is signed by placing the right *A* hand against the center of the chest with palm facing left.

Memory aid: The circular movement suggests the inclusion of others, and the thumb of the *A* hand can represent the self.

Example: We will paint the house *ourselves.*

OUT

Place the downturned fingers of the open right hand in the left *C* hand with the right fingers protruding below the left *C*. Draw the right hand up and out.

Memory aid: Symbolizes coming up *out* of a hole.

Example: They came *out* of the house slowly.

PAIN, ACHE, HURT, INJURY, WOUND

P

Thrust the index fingers toward each other several times. This may be done adjacent to the particular area of the body that is suffering from pain.

Memory aid: Suggests the throbbing of *pain*.

Examples: What kind of *pain* is it? Where are you *hurt*?

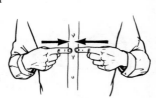

PANTS, SLACKS, TROUSERS

Place the curved open hands just below the waist and move them up to the waist while simultaneously forming *and* hands. *Alternative* (not illustrated): Outline first the left leg and then the right by using both flat hands that point down with palms facing.

Memory aid: The first sign symbolizes pulling up *pants,* and the second outlines each *pant* leg separately.

Example: Your *pants* are baggy at the knees.

PAPER

Strike the heel of the left upturned palm two glancing blows with the heel of the right downturned palm. The right hand moves from right to left to perform the movement.

Memory aid: Can suggest the pressing of pulp to make *paper*.

Example: I need *paper* with narrow lines.

PARENTS

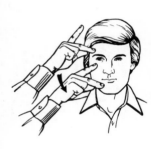

Place the middle finger of the right *P* hand at the right temple, then at the right side of the chin. *Note:* Compare *adult*.

Memory aid: The initial indicates the word, and the two locations refer to the basic male and female positions.

Example: She respected her *parents'* wishes.

PAST, AGO, FORMERLY, LAST, ONCE UPON A TIME, USED TO, PREVIOUSLY, WAS, WERE

Move the right upraised flat hand backward over the right shoulder with palm facing the body. The amount of emphasis with which sign is made can vary depending on the length of time involved. *Note:* See *was* and *were* for alternative signs.

Memory aid: Indicates that which is behind.

Examples: The *past* is forgiven. Richard *was formerly* a lawyer. The prizes were *previously* awarded annually.

PEOPLE

Make inward circles alternately from the sides with both *P* hands. *Note:* Some signers prefer to direct the circles forward.

Memory aid: The *P* hands suggest the word, and the action suggests people milling around.

Example: Many *people* came to the meeting.

PEPPER

Hold the right *O* hand to the front with the *O* pointing down to the left. Shake down to the left a few times.

Memory aid: Symbolizes the use of a *pepper* shaker.

Example: He likes a lot of *pepper* on his food.

PERFECT

Move the middle fingertips of both *P* hands together so that they touch. *Note:* Sometimes this sign can be used interchangeably with the sign for *exact*.

Memory aid: The letter *P*s meet perfectly.

Example: He plays the piano with *perfect precision*.

PERSON

Place both *P* hands forward and move them downward simultaneously.

Memory aid: Suggests outlining the form of another *person*.

Example: Kelly is a fine *person*.

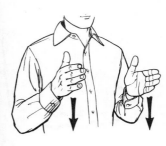

PERSON (personalizing word ending)

Hold both flat open hands to the front with palms facing; then move them down simultaneously.

Memory aid: Suggests outlining the form of another *person*.

Examples: John is our official welcom*er* (sign *welcome* and *person*). There are many Americ*ans* (sign *America* and *person*) who are Christ*ians* (sign *Christ* or *Jesus* and *person*). Malcolm is a clever inven*tor* (sign *invent* and *person*).

PICTURE, PHOTOGRAPH

Hold the right *C* hand close to the face; then move it forward until the thumb side of the right *C* hand is against the left flat palm. The left palm can face either to the right or to the front.

Memory aid: Suggests that a facial likeness is transferred to the flat surface of a *photograph*.

Example: Let me *photograph* you.

PIZZA

Outline the shape of a *Z* in front of the chest with the *P* hand.

Memory aid: Emphasizes the *P* and *Z*s of *pizza*.

Example: Let's have a cheese *pizza* for supper.

PLAN, ARRANGE, ORDER, PREPARE, READY, SYSTEM

Place both flat hands to the front and off to the left with palms facing and fingers pointing forward. Move both hands simultaneously to the right while moving them up and down slightly. *Plan* can be signed with *P* hands, and *ready* with *R* hands.

Memory aid: Suggests placing things in correct sequence.

Examples: What is your *plan*? You need a workable *system*.

PLAY, RECREATION, ROMP

Hold both *Y* hands in front of the chest and pivot them up and down a few times.

Memory aid: The flexibility of the movement suggests that the hands are free to *play*.

Example: Debbie asked her friend to *play* with her.

PLEASE, ENJOY, GRATIFY, LIKE, PLEASURE, WILLING

Make a counterclockwise circle with the right flat hand over the heart. *Willing* can also be signed by placing the right flat hand over the heart and swinging it away from the chest to a palm-up or palm-left position.

Memory aid: Circling the heart indicates a feeling of well-being.

Examples: Please be my friend. It was a *gratifying* experience. It's a *pleasure* to do it for you. I'd be very *willing* to work for you.

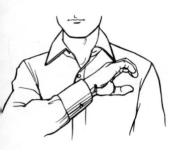

POLICE, COP, SHERIFF

Place the thumb side of the right *C* hand at the left shoulder.

Memory aid: The position at the shoulder indicates those who bear responsibility and authority.

Example: Call the *police*.

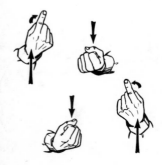

POPCORN

Hold both *S* hands in front with the palms facing up. Flick both index fingers up alternately several times.

Memory aid: Symbolizes the popping of corn kernels.

Example: Please make some *popcorn* for us.

POTATO

Strike the tips of the right curved *V* fingers
on the back of the left downturned *S*
hand.

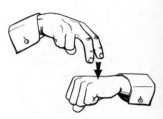

Memory aid: Suggests piercing a *potato*
with a fork.

Example: I like *potatoes* cooked in many
different ways.

PRACTICE, DISCIPLINE,
TRAINING

Rub the knuckles of the right *A* hand back
and forth across the left index finger. A *T*
hand can be used for *training*.

Memory aid: The right hand seems to be
polishing the left index finger to improve
the shine, just as *practice* will improve
quality.

Example: Practice makes perfect.

PROBLEM, DIFFICULTY

Touch the bent knuckles of the two *U* (or
V) hands together and twist in opposite directions while moving downward slightly.

Memory aid: The rubbing knuckles suggest
friction.

Example: He has a *problem* with low
grades.

PROMISE

Touch the lips with the right index finger; then move the right flat hand down and slap it against the thumb and index-finger side of the closed left hand. *Alternative* (not illustrated): Touch the lips with the right index finger; then hold the right hand up with palm facing forward and left flat downturned hand touching right elbow.

Memory aid: The first sign suggests the spoken word is sealed and sure. The second suggests it is backed by an oath.

Example: Paul *promised* he would not tell.

Q

QUESTION

Use the right index finger to outline a question mark in the air. Be sure to include the period.

Memory aid: A question mark obviously indicates a *question.*

Example: It is a difficult *question.*

QUIET, CALM, PEACEFUL, SERENE, SILENT, STILL, TRANQUIL

Touch the lips with the right index finger and move both flat hands down and to the sides with palms facing down. *Note:* The right index finger on the lips is often used by itself for the imperative, *Be quiet!*

Memory aid: These are gestures that indicate *silence* and *peace.*

Example: The sea was *calm.*

RADIO

Cup both hands over the ears.

Memory aid: Suggests the use of *radio* headphones.

Example: I prefer *radio* to television.

RAIN

Touch the mouth with the index finger of the right *W* hand a few times (the sign for *water*). Move both hands down in short stages with wiggling fingers. *Note:* The first part of this sign—the sign for *water*—is not always included.

Memory aid: Suggests water descending.

Example: You'll need your boots because it's *raining*.

READ

Point the right *V* fingers at the left flat palm and move them downward.

Memory aid: The *V* fingers symbolize two eyes *reading* a book.

Example: Walter can *read* aloud flawlessly.

RECENTLY, A WHILE AGO, JUST NOW, LATELY, A SHORT TIME AGO

Place the right curved index finger against the right cheek with the palm and index finger facing back. Move the index finger up and down a few times.

Memory aid: The small movement and the backward direction of the index finger suggest the meaning.

Examples: I *recently* became a vegetarian. Wilbur came by *a short time ago*.

RED

Stroke the lips downward with the right index finger (or *R* fingers).

Memory aid: Suggests *red* lips or lipstick.

Example: Susan chose a *red* carpet.

REFUSE, WON'T

Hold the right *S* (or *A*) hand in a natural position to the front; then move it sharply upward over the right shoulder while simultaneously turning the head to the left at the same time.

Memory aid: Suggests pulling back instead of proceeding in harmony.

Examples: She absolutely *refuses*. He *won't* cooperate.

REMEMBER, MEMORY, RECALL, RECOLLECT

Place the thumb of the right *A* hand on the forehead; then place it on top of the left *A*-hand thumb.

Memory aid: Suggests knowledge that a person can keep on top of.

Examples: Do you *remember* his name? I can't *recall* it.

RESCUE, DELIVER, FREE, INDEPENDENT, LIBERTY, SAFE, REDEEM, SALVATION, SAVIOR

Cross the closed hands on the chest with palms facing in; then rotate them to the sides with palms facing forward. Most signers prefer to initialize each word. For example: Use an *R* for rescue; a *D* for deliver, etc. The observer's understanding is aided by the context.

Memory aid: Suggests breaking a rope tied around the wrists.

Examples: The crew were all *rescued*. The eagle gained its *freedom* at last.

REST, RELAX, UNWIND

Fold the arms in a natural position. Sometimes the *R* hands are used. *Alternative* (not illustrated): Cross the flat (or *R*) hands over the chest.

Memory aid: Both signs suggest natural positions of *rest*.

Example: I need to *relax* for a week.

RIDE (in a vehicle)

Place the right curved *U* fingers in the left *O* hand and move both hands forward.

Memory aid: Suggests a passenger being carried.

Example: Can I *ride* home with you?

RIGHT, ACCURATE, APPROPRIATE, CORRECT, SUITABLE

Point both index fingers forward and bring the little-finger edge of the right hand down onto the thumb edge of the left hand.

Memory aid: The double-handed action can symbolize a person, thing, or circumstance as being doubly *right*.

Examples: You are exactly *right*. The figures are *correct*.

RIGHT (direction)

Move the right *R* hand toward the right.

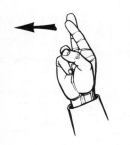

Memory aid: The initial and direction indicate the meaning.

Example: Turn first *right,* then left.

ROCKET, MISSILE

Place the right *R* hand on the back of the closed downturned left hand, and move the right hand forward and up.

Memory aid: Suggests a *rocket* taking off.

Example: The space *rocket* surged with power.

ROOM

Place both flat hands to the front with palms facing; then move the left hand close to the body and the right hand further away with both palms facing the body. This sign can also be done with *R* hands. *Note:* Compare *box*.

Memory aid: The hands outline a rectangular shape.

Example: Our house has six *rooms*.

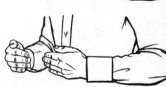

RUN, SPRINT

Place both flat hands palm to palm with the right hand under the left. Slide the right hand quickly forward. *Alternative:* Point both *L* hands forward and hook the right index finger around the left thumb. Wiggle the thumbs and index fingers as both hands move forward quickly.

Memory aid: The quick movement of the first sign suggests the meaning. The alternative sign suggests a relay race.

Example: We'll be late if we don't *run*.

S

SAD, DEJECTED, DESPONDENT, DOWNCAST, FORLORN, SORROWFUL

With palms facing in, bend the head forward slightly while dropping the open hands down the length of the face. Assume a sad expression.

Memory aid: Suggests a sagging expression of melancholy.

Examples: Why are you *sad*? Jack has been very *despondent* lately.

SALT

Tap the right *V* fingers on the left *H* fingers a few times. Sometimes each of the right *V* fingers is used alternately for the tapping movement. Some signers prefer that the left hand also be in the *V* shape.

Memory aid: Suggests the old-fashioned custom of putting *salt* on a knife and tapping it to distribute the *salt*.

Example: This soup has too much *salt*.

SAME, ALIKE, SIMILAR

Bring index fingers together with palms facing down. *Alternative:* Move right *Y* hand either back and forth if referring to self or sideways between two similar persons or things.

Memory aid: The first sign indicates the meaning by the use of two *similar* index fingers. The second suggests the meaning by the thumb and little finger of the same hand being used to point out two persons or two things that are *similar*.

Example: Ted and his brother are *alike*.

SATURDAY

Make a small clockwise circle with the right *S* hand.

Memory aid: The initial suggests the word, and the circular motion suggests the passing of time.

Example: Come on *Saturday*.

SAY, MENTION, REMARK, SPEAK, SPEECH, STATE, TELL

Make a small forward circular movement in front of the mouth with the right index finger.

Memory aid: Suggests a flow of words from the mouth.

Examples: What did Grady *say* about it? The president made some appropriate *remarks*.

SCHOOL

Clap the hands two or three times.

Memory aid: Symbolizes a teacher clapping for attention.

Example: Andrew loves *school*.

SCIENCE, BIOLOGY, CHEMISTRY, EXPERIMENT

Place both *A* hands in front of the shoulders and move them alternately in and down a few times. Use the appropriate initialized hands for *biology, chemistry,* and *experiment.*

Memory aid: Symbolizes the use of test tubes when preparing and testing a solution.

Example: I found *chemistry* difficult to understand.

SEE, PERCEIVE, SIGHT, VISION

With the palm facing in, place the fingertips of the right *V* hand near eyes and move the right hand forward.

Memory aid: The *V* fingers suggest eyes that are actively *seeing.*

Examples: I *saw* you at the store. Being able to *see* is a great gift.

SEX, INTERCOURSE

Hold the left *V* hand to the front with palm facing up. With the palm of the right *V* hand facing down, move it down onto the left *V* hand a few times.

Memory aid: Symbolizes the uniting of two bodies.

Example: *Sex* education begins at home.

SHE, HER

First sign *woman;* then point the index finger forward. If it is obvious that a female is being referred to, the sign for *female* can be omitted.

Memory aid: The signer directs attention by pointing.

Examples: What is *she* going to do? Let me talk to *her.*

SHIRT, BLOUSE

Place the thumb side of the right flat hand on the upper part of the chest with the palm facing down. Move the hand down to the waist while turning it so that the little-finger edge rests against the body with the palm facing up. *Note:* Two hands moving simultaneously may also be used.

Memory aid: Suggests the area covered by a *shirt* or *blouse.*

Example: I need three white *shirts* for the trip.

SHOES, BOOTS

Strike the thumb sides of both closed hands together a few times. To sign *boots,* add the movement of striking the left upper forearm with the little-finger edge of the right flat hand.

Memory aid: Can suggest the clicking of military heels.

Example: These *shoes* fit perfectly.

SHORT (height), SMALL

Place the right bent hand to the front and push down a few times.

Memory aid: The downward action indicates *shortness*.

Example: Brian is still very *short*.

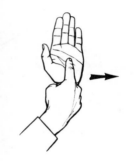

SHOW, DEMONSTRATE, EXPRESS, EXAMPLE, REPRESENT, REVEAL

Hold the left flat hand up with palm facing forward. Place the tip of the right index finger in the left palm and move both hands forward together. All the above words may be initialized with the right hand which is placed in the same position on the left flat palm.

Memory aid: The right hand seems to be *showing* the left hand.

Examples: Sam *demonstrated* his skill at basketball. How can I *express* my appreciation?

SICK, DISEASE, ILL

Place the right middle finger on the forehead and the left middle finger on the stomach. Assume an appropriate facial expression.

Memory aid: The right hand seems to be feeling the temperature of the forehead, while the left hand indicates an area of discomfort.

Example: What is her *disease* called?

SIGNS (deaf language)

Hold both index fingers to the front with the fingers pointing toward each other and the palms facing out. Rotate both index fingers alternately toward the body.

Memory aid: Symbolizes the necessary moving of the hands to engage in *sign* language.

Example: Most deaf *signs* are easy for me to remember.

SING, HYMN, MELODY, MUSIC, SONG

Wave the right flat hand from left to right in front of the left flat hand, which has its palm facing right. The *M* hand can be used for *music*.

Memory aid: Symbolizes the action of a conductor.

Example: Please *sing* for us.

SISTER

First sign *woman;* then point both index fingers forward and bring them together. The latter movement is the sign for *same*.

Memory aid: The two signs combined suggest a female of the same family.

Example: She has two *sisters*.

SIT, BE SEATED, CHAIR, SEAT

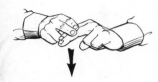

Place the palm side of the right *H* fingers on the back of the left *H* fingers; then move both hands down slightly. The sign for *be seated* is sometimes the natural one of moving both palm-down flat hands with a downward motion in front of the chest. *Note:* Compare *chair*.

Memory aid: Symbolizes a person *sitting* on a chair.

Example: Please *sit* down.

SKIRT

Brush the fingers of both flat open hands downward and outward just below the waist.

Memory aid: Can suggest the smoothing of a *skirt*.

Example: I like the *skirt* you are wearing.

SKY, HEAVENS, SPACE

Hold the right flat hand slightly above head level with the palm facing in. Move it in an arc from left to right. The hand may also be pivoted slightly from left to right during the movement.

Memory aid: Suggests the wide open *space* above.

Example: The *sky* is very blue today.

SLEEP, DOZE, NAP, SIESTA, SLUMBER

Place the palm side of the right open hand in front of the face and move it down to chin level while forming an *and* hand.

Memory aid: Suggests closing the eyes.

Example: A person can have too much *sleep*.

SLOW

Draw the right hand slowly upward over the back of the left hand. Begin near the fingertips and move up to the wrist.

Memory aid: The movement suggests a crawling speed.

Example: Please drive *slowly*.

SMALL, LITTLE (measure, size), TINY

Hold both flat hands to the front with palms facing; then move them closer to each other in short stages. *Note:* Compare *little. Alternatives* (not illustrated): (1) Extend the right index finger and thumb and slowly close the distance. (2) Place the right bent hand at chest level and move it up and down to indicate a short person.

Memory aid: The first two descriptions suggest decreasing space, while the third suggests a person's height.

Example: She bought a very *small* doll.

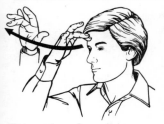

SMART, BRIGHT, BRILLIANT, CLEVER, INTELLIGENT

Touch the forehead with the right middle finger while keeping the other fingers extended. Direct the middle finger outward and upward. The index finger can also be used.

Memory aid: Suggests that *brilliant* thoughts are proceeding from the mind.

Examples: Mark is a *smart* boy. It was a *brilliant* speech.

SMILE, GRIN

Move the fingers (or just the index fingers) upward and backward across the cheeks from the corners of the mouth. Assume an appropriate facial expression.

Memory aid: The upturned mouth suggests the meaning.

Example: Why are you *grinning*?

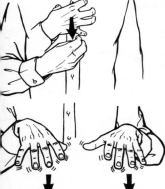

SNOW

Place the fingers and thumb of the right curved hand on the chest; then move it forward while simultaneously forming the *and* hand. Next move both palm-down open hands downward while simultaneously wiggling the fingers. *Note:* This is a combination of the signs for *white* and *rain*.

Memory aid: Suggests something white coming down like rain.

Example: It's *snowing*.

SOCKS, HOSE, STOCKINGS

Point both index fingers down. Rub them up and down against each other alternately.

Memory aid: Suggests the use of needles for hand knitting *socks*.

Example: My *sock* has a hole in it.

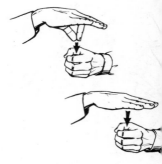

SODA, POP, SODA WATER

Put the thumb and index finger of the right *F* hand into the left *O* hand. Open the right hand and slap the left *O* with it.

Memory aid: Symbolizes inserting a cork into a bottle and forcing it down.

Example: There are many kinds of *sodas* these days.

SOME, PART, PORTION, SECTION

Place the little-finger edge of the slightly curved right hand onto the left flat palm. Pull the right hand toward self while forming a flat right hand.

Memory aid: Suggests the action of separating a *portion* for oneself.

Examples: Give me *some*. This *section* is reserved for me.

SOMETIMES, OCCASIONALLY, ONCE IN A WHILE, SELDOM

Hold the left flat hand at chest level with palm facing right. Touch the left palm with the right index fingertip; then move the right index finger upward to a vertical position. Repeat after a slight pause.

Memory aid: The slow movement indicates irregularity.

Examples: Pete *sometimes* comes early. I travel only *occasionally*. *Once in a while* I create something worthwhile. Jane *seldom* joins in the group.

SON

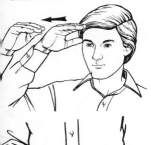

First sign *man;* then move the right flat hand with palm facing up into the crook of the bent left elbow.

Memory aid: Indicates a male baby cradled in the arms.

Example: They have one *son*.

SOON, BRIEF, SHORT (length of time)

Cross the fingers of both *H* hands and rub the right *H* hand back and forth over the left index finger from fingertip to knuckle.

Memory aid: The *shortness* of the movement suggests the meaning.

Examples: Gerald will arrive *soon*. Please be *brief*. We held a *short* conversation.

SORROW, APOLOGY, REGRET

Rotate the right *A* (or *S*) hand in a few counterclockwise circles over the heart.

Memory aid: Rubbing the heart suggests inner feelings of *sorrow*.

Examples: I'm *sorry* about your election defeat. Please accept my sincere *apology*.

SOUTH

Move the *S* hand downward with palm facing forward.

Memory aid: Indicates direction.

Example: The *south* wind is blowing.

SPOON

Lift the right curved *H* fingers upward toward the mouth a few times from the palm of the slightly curved left hand.

Memory aid: Symbolizes use of a *spoon*.

Example: I need a clean *spoon*.

SPRING, GROW, MATURE

Open the fingers of the right *and* hand as they pass up through the left *C* hand.

Memory aid: Suggests young shoots coming up out of the ground.

Example: Martha always looked forward to *spring*.

STAND UP, ARISE, GET UP, RISE

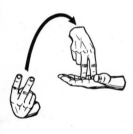

Begin with the right *V* fingers pointing up and the palm facing in. Make an arc with the *V* fingers until they rest in an upright position on the left upturned palm.

Memory aid: The *V* fingers represent a person's legs.

Examples: Please *stand up*. What time shall we *get up* tomorrow?

START, BEGIN, COMMENCE, INITIATE

Hold the left flat hand forward with the palm facing right. Place the tip of the right index finger between the left index and middle fingers, then twist in a clockwise direction once or twice.

Memory aid: Can symbolize turning the ignition key to *start* a car.

Examples: Her car will not *start*. Let's *begin* the lesson.

STOP, CEASE, HALT

Bring the little-finger side of the right flat hand down sharply at right angles on the left palm.

Memory aid: Suggests a barrier to *stop* progress.

Examples: Stop it! The soldiers *halted* on their march.

STORY, TALE

Link the thumbs and index fingers of both *F* hands and pull them apart several times. *Note:* Compare *sentence.*

Memory aid: Suggests many sentences linked together to make a *story.*

Example: What is your favorite childhood *story*?

STRONG, MIGHTY, POWERFUL

Move both *S* hands firmly forward and downward. *Alternative:* Describe a downward arc with the right curved hand from the left shoulder to the inside of the left elbow. *Note:* Compare *authority.*

Memory aid: The clenched fists of the first sign suggest *strength,* and the action for the alternative sign suggests a *powerful* biceps muscle.

Example: He gave the ax a *mighty* swing.

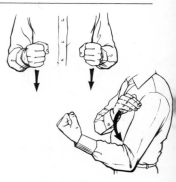

STUDY

Point the right open fingers toward the left flat hand. Move the right hand back and forth a short distance from the left while simultaneously wiggling the right fingers.

Memory aid: The right hand seems to be *studying* the left hand intently. The left hand can represent a book.

Example: How many hours a day do you *study*?

STUPID, DULL, DUMB, DUNCE

Knock the *A* (or *S*) hand against the forehead a few times with the palm facing in.

Memory aid: Knocking on the head can indicate a figuratively hollow interior.

Examples: Some rules seem *stupid*. That's a *dumb* question.

SUCCEED, ACCOMPLISH, PROSPER

Point both index fingers toward each other or toward the head; then move them upward while simultaneously making little forward circles. End with both index fingers pointing up and palms facing forward.

Memory aid: Suggests increasingly higher stages.

Example: He is a *successful* marathon runner.

SUMMER

Draw the curved right index finger across the forehead from left to right.

Memory aid: Symbolizes the wiping of perspiration.

Example: This *summer* Bob is going to camp.

SUN, SUNSHINE

Point the right index finger forward just above head level and make a clockwise circle. To sign *sunshine,* add the action of either one or both *and* hands moving down and across the body while simultaneously forming open hands.

Memory aid: Symbolizes the position, shape, and rays of the sun.

Example: The *sunshine* streamed into the window.

SUNDAY

Place both flat hands to the front with palms facing forward; then move them simultaneously in opposite-direction circles. The circles may be made in either direction.

Memory aid: The hand movements suggest reverential worship.

Example: I usually rest on *Sundays.*

SURPRISE, AMAZE, ASTONISH, ASTOUND

Place both closed hands at the temples with index fingertips and thumb tips touching. Flick both index fingers up simultaneously.

Memory aid: Suggests wide-eyed *surprise*.

Examples: It was a *surprise* party. The result was *astonishing*.

SWEET

Brush the right fingertips downward over the lips. Sometimes this is done on the chin.

Memory aid: Suggests licking something *sweet* on the fingers.

Example: I love to eat *sweet* things.

SWEETHEART, BEAU, LOVER

Bring the knuckles of both *A* hands together with palms facing inward; then raise and lower both thumbs simultaneously.

Memory aid: Suggests two lovebirds billing and cooing.

Example: She had quite a few *sweethearts*.

SWIMMING

Place the slightly curved hands to the front with the backs of the hands partially facing each other and the fingers pointing forward. Move the hands simultaneously forward and to the sides.

Memory aid: The action simulates the breaststroke.

Example: Swimming regularly will keep your muscles well toned.

TABLE

T

Place both arms to the front in a similar position to that of folding them, but put the right forearm over the left. The right flat hand can pat the top of the left forearm a few times.

Memory aid: Can suggest resting the arms on a *table* surface.

Example: I love antique *tables*.

TAKE

Place the right open hand forward and draw it into the chest while simultaneously forming a closed hand.

Memory aid: Symbolizes reaching out and *taking* something.

Example: We *took* everything.

TALK, COMMUNICATE, CONVERSATION, DIALOGUE, INTERVIEW

Move both index fingers back and forth from the lips alternately. Use *C* hands for *communicate* and *conversation, D* hands for *dialogue,* and *I* hands for *interview.*

Memory aid: Suggests the words coming and going in a *conversation.*

Example: Our *conversation* was profitable.

TALL

Place the right index finger on the left flat palm and move it straight up.

Memory aid: The upward movement suggests the meaning.

Example: My cousin is very *tall.*

TASTE

Touch the tip of the tongue with the right middle finger. The other fingers of the right open hand are extended.

Memory aid: The finger is giving the tongue a sample *taste.*

Example: What does the flavor *taste* like?

TEACH, EDUCATE, INDOCTRINATE, INSTRUCT

Position both open *and* hands at the front and sides of the head, then move them forward while simultaneously forming closed *and* hands.

Memory aid: Suggests pulling out knowledge from the mind and presenting it to others.

Example: Tim will *instruct* you correctly.

TEETH

Move the tip of the right index finger sideways across the front teeth.

Memory aid: The *teeth* are indicated by pointing to them.

Example: Her *teeth* are healthy.

TELEPHONE, CALL

Position the *Y* hand at the right of the face so that the thumb is near the ear and the little finger near the mouth.

Memory aid: The natural position for using the *telephone*.

Example: What is your *phone* number?

TELEVISION

Fingerspell T—V.

Memory aid: The initials indicate the word.

Example: Do you have a color *television*?

THAN

Hold the left flat or curved hand to the front with palm facing down. Brush the index-finger edge of the right flat hand down off the fingertips of the left hand.

Memory aid: The right hand is both above and below the left hand, thus showing a comparison.

Example: Jim is a better craftsman *than* Pete.

THANKS, THANK YOU, YOU'RE WELCOME

Touch the lips with the fingertips of one or both flat hands, then move the hands forward until the palms are facing up. It is natural to smile and nod the head while making this sign.

Memory aid: A natural expression of affection used when one is grateful.

Example: *Thanks* for your concern.

THAT

Place the right downturned *Y* hand on the left upturned palm. *Note:* Omit the sign for *that* when it is a conjunctive, as in the sentence, It is good *that* you trust me.

Memory aid: *That* is often used in relation to either asking or answering a question. The *Y* hand suggests the interrogative *why*.

Example: What's the name of *that* building?

THERE

Point with the right index finger when being specific. For a more general reference, move the right flat hand to the right with palm facing forward.

Memory aid: A gesture indicating location.

Example: The oak tree is over *there*.

THESE, THEM, THEY, THOSE

Point the right index finger forward or in the direction of the persons or objects referred to, then move it to the right.

Memory aid: The signer directs attention by pointing.

Examples: I see *them* over there. *They* are in a jubilant mood today.

THINK, CONSIDER, REFLECT, SPECULATE

Make a counterclockwise circle with the right index finger just in front of the forehead. This can be done simultaneously with two hands if more intensity of meaning is required.

Memory aid: The circular motion indicates action in the mind.

Examples: I am *thinking*. Nancy *reflected* upon her past.

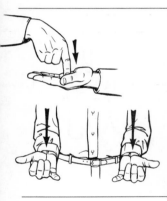

THIS

Put the right index fingertip into the palm of the flat left hand if something specific is indicated. Drop both *Y* (or flat) hands together with palms facing up if something more abstract is indicated. Sometimes the right *Y* hand by itself is moved downward with palm facing down.

Memory aid: The right index finger points to an object in the left hand. Or both hands seem to be holding something for others to see.

Examples: Specific—*This* is my pencil. Abstract—What is *this* message you have?

THURSDAY

Make a small clockwise circle with the right *H* hand. *Note:* This is sometimes signed with the manual *T* and *H*, with or without rotation.

Memory aid: The initial suggests the word, and the circular motion suggests the passing of time.

Example: Come on *Thursday*.

TIME, CLOCK, WATCH

The right curved index fingertip is made to tap the back of the left wrist a few times.

Memory aid: An obvious reference to a *wristwatch*.

Examples: What is the *time*? My *watch* is a present from Sam.

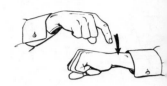

TIME (abstract), TIMES, AGE, EPOCH, ERA, SEASON

Rotate the thumb (or knuckle side) of the right *T* hand in a clockwise circle on the left flat palm. *Note:* Use an *S* right hand to sign *season*.

Memory aid: The initial indicates the word, and the action symbolizes the truth that the clock stops for no one.

Example: Times are unpredictable.

TIRED, EXHAUSTED, FATIGUED, WEARY

Place the fingertips of both bent hands on the upper chest, then pivot the hands downward while maintaining contact with the chest. The fingertips point upward in the final position.

Memory aid: Suggests that the body is ready to drop in *exhaustion*.

Example: Joe *wearily* dragged himself up the stairs.

TO (preposition), TOWARD

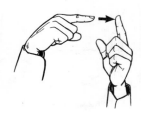

Hold the left index finger up and move the right index finger toward it until the fingertips touch. *Note:* Do not touch fingertips when signing *toward*.

Memory aid: Suggests the concept of moving closer.

Examples: He's leaving to go *to* Nebraska. The basketball team was headed *toward* certain victory.

TOAST

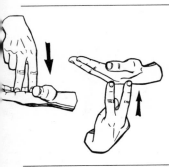

Thrust the right *V* fingers into the left palm; then into the back of the left flat hand.

Memory aid: Suggests the old-fashioned method of using a special long fork to *toast* bread in front of a fire.

Example: I love marmalade on *toast*.

TODAY

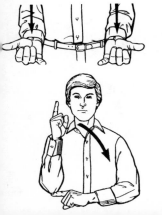

Drop both *Y* (or flat) hands together in front of the chest. Point the left index finger to the right with palm down. Rest the right elbow on the left index finger and point the right index upward. Move the right arm in a partial arc across the body from right to left. This sign can also be done by combining either *now* and *day*, or *this* and *day*.

Memory aid: The horizontal left arm indicates the horizon, while the right arm symbolizes the movement of the sun.

Example: We must finish *today*.

TOGETHER, ACCOMPANY

Place the knuckles of both *A* hands together and move them in a forward semi-circle to the left.

Memory aid: Suggests two people or things moving *together*.

Example: Families need to be *together*.

TOILET, BATHROOM, RESTROOM

Shake the right *T* hand in front of the chest with the palm facing forward. *Restroom* can also be signed by pointing the right *R* hand forward and moving it in a short arc to the right.

Memory aid: The shaking motion suggests the need to meet a physical requirement.

Example: May I use your *restroom*?

TOMORROW

Touch the right *A* thumb on the right cheek or chin area; then make a forward arc.

Memory aid: The forward movement indicates the future.

Example: What shall we do *tomorrow*?

TREE, BRANCH, FOREST, WOODS

Place the right elbow in the left palm with the right fingers pointing up. Pivot the right wrist and wiggle the fingers. Initials can be used for *branch, forest,* and *woods.*

Memory aid: The forearm symbolizes a *tree* trunk, while the moving hand and fingers suggest the *branches* and leaves.

Example: Climbing *trees* can be dangerous.

TRUE, AUTHENTIC, GENUINE, REAL, REALLY, SINCERE, SURE, TRUTH, VALID

With palm facing left, move the right index finger in a forward arc from the lips.

Memory aid: Symbolizes *true* and straight-forward communication.

Examples: We need to know the *true* story. It's a *sure* thing.

TUESDAY

Make a small clockwise circle with the right *T* hand.

Memory aid: The initial suggests the word, and the circular motion suggests the passing of time.

Example: Come on *Tuesday.*

UGLY, HOMELY

U

Cross the index fingers just below the nose with the remaining fingers closed; then bend the index fingers as the hands are pulled apart to the sides. Sometimes only one hand is used. Assume an appropriate facial expression by frowning.

Memory aid: Suggests facial features that are distorted and pulled out of shape.

Example: She is unfortunate to be so *homely*.

UNCLE

With the palm facing forward, place the right *U* hand close to the right temple and shake back and forth from the wrist.

Memory aid: The initial *U* is placed near the *male* sign position.

Example: My *uncle* was an excellent boxer in his youth.

UNDERSTAND, COMPREHEND

With the palm facing in, flick the right index finger up vertically in front of the forehead. *Alternative* (not illustrated): A more formal sign touches the forehead with the *S* hand before flicking up the index finger.

Memory aid: Both signs suggest a figurative light of *understanding* coming on in the mind.

Example: Are you sure you *understand*?

UNTIL

Hold the left index finger up with palm facing inward. Move the right index finger in a slow forward arc until it touches the tip of the left index finger.

Memory aid: Wait *until* contact is made.

Example: Do your best *until* I get there.

UP

Hold up the right index finger with palm facing forward and move it up slightly. This word is sometimes fingerspelled.

Memory aid: Pointing upward.

Example: Can you reach *up* to that shelf?

USE, USEFUL, UTILIZE

With the palm facing forward, make a clockwise circle with the right *U* hand.

Memory aid: The letter *U* is put to work.

Example: Please *use* this towel.

VACATION, HOLIDAY, LEISURE

V

Place both thumbs at the armpits and wiggle all the fingers.

Memory aid: A common symbol of *leisure*.

Example: She goes on *vacation* next week.

VERY

With the palms facing in, touch the fingertips of both *V* hands; then draw both hands apart to the sides.

Memory aid: The initial plus the same movement as is used for *much* indicate the meaning.

Example: That is a *very* nice dress.

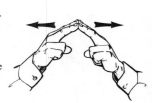

VISIT

Hold both *V* hands up with palms facing in. Rotate them forward alternately.

Memory aid: The action symbolizes a mingling of people among each other.

Example: She *visited* me yesterday.

VOICE, VOCAL

Draw the back of the right *V* fingers up the neck and forward under the chin.

Memory aid: The initial indicates the word, and the action shows the location.

Example: John has a powerful bass *voice*.

W

WAIT, PENDING

With palms facing up, hold both curved open hands up to the left with the right hand behind the left. Wiggle all the fingers.

Memory aid: The wiggling fingers suggest impatience.

Example: He *waited* four hours before leaving.

WALK, STEP

Hold both flat hands in front with palms down; then imitate walking by moving each hand forward alternately.

Memory aid: Symbolizes the movement of feet.

Example: Please *walk* with me.

WANT, COVET, DESIRE

With palms facing up, move both open curved hands toward self a few times. *Note:* Compare *don't want*.

Memory aid: Suggests pulling something toward self.

Examples: Jackie *wants* to come and see you. I *covet* your good looks.

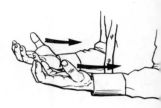

WARN, CAUTION

Pat the back of the left flat hand with the right flat hand a few times.

Memory aid: Suggests slapping the hand as a disciplinary measure.

Example: Calvin was *warned* of the dangers.

WAS

Hold the right *W* hand in front with palm facing left. Move it backward to a position by the side of the neck or cheek, and at the same time change from a *W* to an *S* hand. *Note:* See *past*.

Memory aid: Backward movement indicates the past.

Example: Robert *was* always bright in English.

WASH

Rub the knuckles of both closed hands together with circular movements.

Memory aid: Suggests *washing* clothes by hand.

Example: Your jersey needs *washing*.

WATER

Touch the mouth with the index finger of the right *W* hand a few times.

Memory aid: The initial indicates the word, and the movement points to the location for drinking.

Example: The *water* level at the dam is high.

WAY, AVENUE, HIGHWAY, PATH, ROAD, STREET

Hold both flat hands with palms facing; then move them forward together while simultaneously winding from side to side. *Note:* All these words may be signed by using the initial. Thus, *way* could be signed with *W* hands, and so on.

Memory aid: Symbolizes the direction of a *road*.

Example: Which *highway* will you travel?

WE, US

Touch the right index finger on the right
shoulder; then move it in a forward semi-
circle until it touches the left shoulder.
Often the W or U hand is used instead of
the index finger to indicate either *we* or *us*
respectively.

Memory aid: The circular movement suggests others in addition to self.

Examples: We will see you soon. Allow *us*
to come in.

WEATHER

Hold both W hands to the front with
palms facing; then pivot them up and
down from the wrists.

Memory aid: The initials indicate the
word, and the action indicates the change-
able nature of *weather*.

Example: What's the *weather* forecast for
tomorrow?

WEDDING

Point the fingers of both flat hands down
from the wrists in the front. Swing the
hands toward each other until the left fingers and thumb grasp the right fingers.

Memory aid: Suggests a bride and groom
joining hands.

Example: Becky and Tom's *wedding* was
very elaborate.

WEDNESDAY

Make a small clockwise circle with the right *W* hand.

Memory aid: The initial suggests the word, and the circular motion suggests the passing of time.

Example: Come on *Wednesday*.

WEEK, NEXT WEEK, LAST WEEK

Move the right index-finger hand across the left flat palm in a forward movement. For *next week*, let the right hand continue beyond the left hand and point forward. For *last week*, let the right hand continue in an upward-backward direction to the right shoulder. *Week* and *past* can also be used to sign *last week*.

Memory aid: The five fingers of the left hand plus the thumb and index finger of the right make seven, thus symbolizing a *week*.

Example: This has been a hectic *week*.

WELCOME

Position the right flat hand forward and to the right with the palm facing left. Sweep the hand in toward the body until the palm is facing in front of the abdomen.

Memory aid: A common gesture of politeness and acceptance.

Example: You are *welcome* here.

WERE

Hold the right *W* hand slightly to the front with the palm facing left. Move it backward to a position at the side of the neck or cheek while simultaneously changing from a *W* to an *R* hand. *Note:* See *past*.

Memory aid: Backward movement indicates the past.

Example: In 1956 they *were* in college.

WEST

Move the *W* hand to the left.

Memory aid: Indicates direction.

Example: The *western* sky was aflame.

WET, DRENCH, SATURATE, SOAK

Tap the right side of the mouth with the index finger of the right *W* hand a few times. Hold both curved open hands to the front with palms facing up; then move the hands slowly down while simultaneously forming *and* hands. *Note:* This sign is a combination of *water* and *soft*.

Memory aid: Suggests the feeling of wet fingers.

Example: Your feet are absolutely *soaked*.

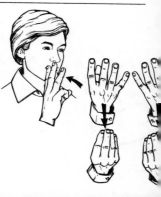

WHAT

Pass the tip of the right index finger down over the left flat hand from index to little finger.

Memory aid: The fingers of the left hand suggest alternative ideas to choose from.

Example: What is today's date?

WHEN

Hold the left index finger upright with the palm facing right. Make a clockwise circle around the left index finger with the right index finger.

Memory aid: The right index finger seems to be wondering *when* it can stop circling the left index finger.

Example: When will you be ready to go out?

WHERE

Hold the right index finger up with the palm facing forward. Shake it rapidly back and forth from left to right.

Memory aid: Suggests a rapid looking and searching from side to side.

Example: Where is my book?

WHICH, EITHER, WHETHER

With the palms facing, move the *A* hands alternately up and down in front of the chest.

Memory aid: Suggests two or more things being compared.

Example: Which team do you think will win?

WHITE

Place the fingers and thumb of the right curved hand on the chest; then move it forward while simultaneously forming the *and* hand.

Memory aid: Can suggest reference to a clean *white* shirt.

Example: Buy some *white* sheets when you go to the store.

WHO, WHOM

Make a counterclockwise circle in front of the lips with the right index finger.

Memory aid: Attention is drawn to the lips as they form the word shape.

Examples: Who is there? To *whom* should I make my request?

WHY

Touch the forehead with the fingers of the right hand; then move forward while simultaneously forming the *Y* hand with the palm facing in.

Memory aid: The *Y* hand coming from the mind suggests a question by its phonetic link to *why*.

Example: Why do you want to leave college?

WIFE

First sign *woman;* then clasp the hands in a natural position with the right hand above the left. The latter is the sign for *marriage.*

Memory aid: Indicates a married female.

Examples: John's *wife* is a nurse. All their *wives* are invited.

WILL (verb), SHALL, WOULD

Place the right flat hand opposite the right temple or cheek with the palm facing in. Move the hand straight ahead.

Memory aid: The forward movement indicates future intention.

Examples: Tom *will* come on Saturday. We *shall* overcome! I *would* love to be there.

WINTER

Hold up both *S* hands in front of the chest and shake them.

Memory aid: Suggests a person shivering in the cold.

Example: Last *winter* was unusually mild.

WISH

With the palm facing in, draw the right *C* hand down the chest from just below the neck. *Note*: Compare *hungry*.

Memory aid: The *C* hand suggests a craving, such as for food.

Example: I *wish* I had more money.

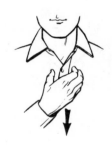

WITH, WITHOUT

To sign *with*, join the two *A* hands with palms facing. To sign *without*, begin with the same basic position; then separate the hands and move them outward while simultaneously forming open hands.

Memory aid: The two hands are first *with* each other and then *without* each other.

Examples: Come *with* me. We must go *without* luxuries.

WOMAN, FEMALE

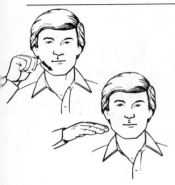

Trace the right jawbone from ear to chin with the palm side of the right *A* thumb. Some add the motion of moving the right flat downturned hand away from the head to indicate height when signing *woman*.

Memory aid: The thumb follows the action of the old-fashioned bonnet string.

Examples: This cat is *female*. That *woman* was here first.

WONDERFUL, EXCELLENT, FANTASTIC, GREAT, MARVELOUS, SPLENDID

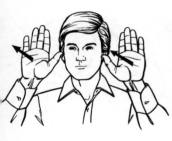

Move the flat open hands up and forward a few times with the palms facing out.

Memory aid: A gesture symbolizing an attitude of awe that is used in some forms of religious worship.

Example: You are a *fantastic* cook.

WORD

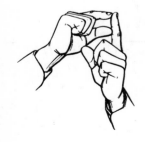

Hold the left index finger up with palm facing left; then place the thumb and index finger of the right *Q* hand against it.

Memory aid: Symbolizes that a *word* is just a small section of a sentence.

Example: Jill is fascinated by the origin of *words*.

WORK, JOB, LABOR, TASK

With the palms facing down, tap the wrist of the right *S* hand on the wrist of the left *S* hand a few times.

Memory aid: Suggests the action of a hammer.

Example: Sam needs a new *job*.

WORRY, ANXIOUS, FRET

Rotate both flat or slightly curved hands in front of the head in opposite directions.

Memory aid: Suggests problems being heaped upon the mind.

Examples: Joe *worries* about his job a lot. Please don't *fret* about it.

WOULD

With the palm facing left, place the right *W* hand in an upright position close to the side of the right cheek. Move the hand straight forward while simultaneously changing from a *W* to a *D* hand.

Memory aid: Forward movement indicates positive intention.

Example: Would you like to eat now?

WRITE

Touch the right index finger and thumb with the other fingers closed; then move the right hand horizontally across the flat left palm with a slight wavy motion.

Memory aid: Symbolizes *writing* on paper.

Example: She *writes* children's stories.

WRONG, ERROR, FAULT, MISTAKE

Place the *Y* hand on the chin with the palm facing in.

Memory aid: The *Y* hand is normally shown with palm facing out, so this position suggests a *mistake*.

Example: Please forgive my *mistake*.

X

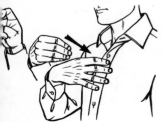

X RAY

Hold the right *X* hand up with palm facing forward; then form an *O* position and twist the hand until the palm faces self. Open the hand as it is moved toward the chest.

Memory aid: The initial indicates the word, and the action suggests *X rays* penetrating the body.

Example: The doctor decided to *X-ray* my ankle.

YEAR, LAST YEAR, NEXT YEAR

Move the right *S* hand in a complete forward circle around the left *S* hand and come to rest with the right *S* hand on top of the left. Repeat the sign for the plural. To sign *last year*, complete the basic sign for *year*; then point the right index finger backward over the right shoulder. To sign *next year*, complete the basic sign for *year*, then point the right index finger forward.

Memory aid: The movement of the right hand suggests the earth's revolution around the sun.

Example: What *year* were you born?

YES

Nod the right *S* hand up and down with palm facing forward.

Memory aid: Suggests a nodding head.

Example: My answer is *yes*.

YESTERDAY

With the palm facing forward, place the thumb of the right *A* (or *Y*) hand on the right side of the chin. Move in a backward arc toward the ear.

Memory aid: The backward movement indicates the past.

Example: *Yesterday* was exciting.

YOU

Point the right index finger to the person being addressed. Or, if referring to several people, make a sweeping motion from left to right.

Memory aid: The person being pointed to clearly understands the reference to self.

Examples: You are right. *You* must play as a united team.

YOUNG, ADOLESCENT, YOUTH

Place the fingertips of both curved hands on the upper chest and quickly pivot them upward from the wrists several times. *Note:* Compare *life*.

Memory aid: Symbolizes a fast pace of life and *youthful* exuberance.

Example: We all experience the joys and trials of *youth*.

YOURSELF, HERSELF, HIMSELF, ITSELF, ONESELF, THEMSELVES, YOURSELVES

Hold the right *A* hand thumb up and make several short forward movements in the direction of the person or object referred to.

Memory aid: The jerking movement can suggest the individual nature of persons or things.

Examples: Joe can understand *himself* much better lately. The car is rolling by *itself*.

ZOO

Z

Hold the left flat open hand up with palm facing forward. Trace the letter Z across the front of the left hand with the right index finger. This sign is often finger-spelled.

Memory aid: The initial indicates the word, and the open left hand suggests the bars on animal cages.

Example: I've always found *zoos* interesting.

Main Entry and Synonym Index

THIS INDEX is a list of all main entries (in **bold face** type) and the synonyms (in light face type) that are to be found following the main entries in the dictionary. The sign-language student will find this list an invaluable aid to versatility of expression. It will also assist the student in locating a basic sign when he or she can think only of a synonym.

Abhor   *See* Hate.
Ability   *See* Can.
Able   *See* Can.
Above
Above (comparative degree)
Absent   *See* Gone.
Accompany   *See* Together.
Accomplish   *See* Succeed.
Accord   *See* Agree.
Accurate   *See* Right.
Ache   *See* Pain.
Acquire   *See* Get.
Action   *See* Do.
Add
Address   *See* Live.
Adjacent   *See* Near.
Admire   *See* Like.
Adolescent   *See* Young.
Afraid   *See* Frightened.
After
After a While   *See* Later.
Afternoon
Afterward   *See* Later.
Again
Against
Age   *See* Old.
Ago   *See* Past.
Agree
Aid   *See* Help.
Algebra   *See* Mathematics.
Alike   *See* Same.
All
All Day   *See* Day.
All Night   *See* Night.

All Right
Alphabet   *See* Fingerspelling.
Already   *See* Finish.
Although   *See* Anyway. But.
Always
Am
Amaze   *See* Surprise.
America
Amusing   *See* Fun.
Ancient   *See* Old.
And
Anger
Animal
Answer
Antique   *See* Old.
Anxious   *See* Worry.
Any
Anybody   *See* Any.
Anyhow   *See* Anyway.
Anyone   *See* Any.
Anything   *See* Any.
Anyway
Apology   *See* Sorrow.
Appetite   *See* Hunger.
Apple
Appropriate   *See* Right.
Are   *See* Am.
Arise   *See* Stand Up.
Arouse   *See* Awake. Excite.
Arrange   *See* Plan.
Artificial   *See* False.
As
Ask
A Short Time Ago   *See* Recently.

Has *See* Have.
Hate
Have
Have To *See* Must.
He
Healthy
Hear *See* Ear.
Hearing
Hearing Aid
Heart (physical)
Heavens *See* Sky.
Hell *See* Fire.
Hello *See* Hi.
Help
Her *See* His.
Her *See* She.
Here
Herself *See* Yourself.
Hi
Highway *See* Way.
Hilarious *See* Fun.
Him *See* He.
Himself *See* Yourself.
His
Holiday *See* Vacation.
Home
Homely *See* Ugly.
Horse
Hose *See* Socks.
Hospital
Hot
Hour
How
However *See* But.
Huge *See* Large.
Humorous *See* Fun.
Hunger
Hurry
Hurt *See* Pain.
Husband
Hustle *See* Hurry.
Hymn *See* Sing.

I
Ice Cream
If
Ill *See* Sick.

Immediate *See* Now.
Immediately *See* Fast.
Immense *See* Large.
Imperative *See* Must.
Important
Impossible *See* Cannot.
Improve
In
Incapable *See* Cannot.
Independent *See* Rescue.
Indoctrinate *See* Teach.
Inexpensive *See* Cheap.
Infant *See* Baby.
Initiate *See* Start.
Injury *See* Pain.
Instruct *See* Teach.
Intelligence *See* Know.
Intelligent *See* Smart.
Intercourse *See* Sex.
Interest
Interpret
Interview *See* Talk.
Into *See* In.
Is *See* Am.
Itself *See* Yourself.

Jacket *See* Coat.
Jealous
Job *See* Work.
Joy *See* Happy.
Just Now *See* Recently.

Keep
Kid
Kiss
Kitchen
Knife
Know
Knowledge *See* Know.

Labor *See* Work.
Language
Large
Last
Last *See* Past.
Lasting *See* Continue.
Lastly *See* Last.

Pleasure *See* Please.
Plump *See* Fat.
Plural *See* Many.
Police
Pop *See* Soda.
Popcorn
Portion *See* Some.
Possess *See* Have.
Possible *See* Can.
Possibly *See* May.
Potato
Powerful *See* Strong.
Practice
Precious *See* Important.
Prepare *See* Plan.
Present *See* Gift.
Present *See* Now.
Pretty *See* Beautiful.
Previously *See* Past.
Price *See* Cost.
Probably *See* May.
Problem
Promise
Prosper *See* Succeed.
Protest *See* Complain.
Pseudo *See* False.
Psychiatry *See* Doctor.
Purchase *See* Buy.
Pure *See* Clean.

Question
Quick *See* Fast.
Quiet

Radio
Rage *See* Anger.
Rain
Rapid *See* Fast.
Read
Ready *See* Plan.
Real *See* True.
Really *See* True.
Recall *See* Remember.
Receive *See* Get.
Recently
Reckless *See* Careless.
Recognize *See* Know.

Recollect *See* Remember.
Recreation *See* Play.
Red
Redeem *See* Rescue.
Reflect *See* Think.
Refuse
Regardless *See* Anyway.
Regret *See* Sorrow.
Relax *See* Rest.
Remark *See* Say.
Remember
Repeat *See* Again.
Reply *See* Answer.
Represent *See* Show.
Request *See* Ask.
Rescue
Reside *See* Live.
Respond *See* Answer.
Rest
Restroom *See* Toilet.
Retire *See* Leave.
Reveal *See* Show.
Reverse Interpret *See* Interpret.
Reward *See* Gift.
Ride (in a vehicle)
Ridiculous *See* Foolish.
Right
Right (direction)
Rise *See* Stand Up.
Rival *See* Enemy.
Road *See* Way.
Robust *See* Healthy.
Rocket
Romp *See* Play.
Room
Rotten *See* Lousy
Run
Rush *See* Hurry.

Sad
Safe *See* Rescue.
Salt
Salvation *See* Rescue.
Same
Saturate *See* Wet.
Saturday
Savior *See* Rescue.

Stupid
Subdue *See* Conquer.
Subsequently *See* Later.
Substance *See* Any.
Succeed
Suddenly *See* Fast.
Sugar *See* Candy.
Suit *See* Clothes.
Suitable *See* Right.
Summer
Summon *See* Call.
Sun
Sunday
Sunshine *See* Sun.
Supervise *See* Keep.
Supper *See* Dinner.
Sure *See* True.
Surgeon *See* Doctor.
Surprise
Sweet
Sweetheart
Swift *See* Fast.
Swimming
System *See* Plan.

Table
Take
Tale *See* Story.
Talk
Tall
Task *See* Work.
Taste
Tax *See* Cost.
Teach
Teardrop *See* Cry.
Tears *See* Cry.
Tedious *See* Boring.
Teeth
Telephone
Television
Tell *See* Say.
Terrified *See* Frightened.
Textbook *See* Book.
Than
Thanks
Thank You *See* Thanks.
That
Their *See* His.
Them *See* These.

Themselves *See* Yourself.
There
These
They *See* These.
Thing *See* Any.
Think
This
Those *See* These.
Thoughtless *See* Careless.
Thrill *See* Excite.
Thursday
Time
Time (abstract)
Tiny *See* Small
Tired
To (preposition)
Toast
Today
Together
Toilet
Tomorrow
Tongue *See* Language.
Toward *See* To (preposition).
Training *See* Practice.
Tranquil *See* Quiet.
Translate *See* Interpret.
Tree
Tricycle *See* Bicycle.
Trigonometry *See* Mathematics.
Triumph *See* Celebration.
Trousers *See* Pants.
True
Truth *See* True.
Try *See* Attempt.
Tuesday

Ugly
Unable *See* Cannot.
Uncle
Under *See* Below.
Under *See* Below.
   (comparative degree).
Understand
Unlike *See* Different.
Until
Unwind *See* Rest.
Up
Us *See* We.

If you enjoyed this book,
you'll also want to order

The Perigee Visual Dictionary of Signing
ISBN 0-399-50863-5

A comprehensive signing dictionary containing over
1,200 signs of American Sign Language!

For your convenience, use the coupon to order.
Attach an additional page if necessary.
These books are also available at your local bookstore
or wherever paperback books are sold.

G. P. Putnam's Sons
390 Murray Hill Parkway, Dept. B
East Rutherford, New Jersey 07073

Please send me _____ copies of *The Perigee Visual Dictionary of
Signing* (SBN 399-50863-5) at $9.95 each.

Enclosed is my ☐ check ☐ money order.
Please charge my ☐ Visa ☐ MasterCard.
Card # _____

Expiration date _____

Name _____

Address _____

City _____ State ____ Zip _____

Signature as on charge card _____

Subtotal	$_____
Postage & Handling	$___1.50
Sales Tax	$_____
Total	$_____

Please allow 4 to 6 weeks for delivery.